A Pocketful of Change

Organize Your Small Charitable Gifts for Big Results

by

Gail R. Shapiro

Published by BookLocker.com, Inc., St. Petersburg, Florida.

Printed on acid-free paper.

BookLocker.com, Inc.
2017

First Edition

Dedication

To Arline and Harold Shapiro, for teaching me about giving.

DISCLAIMER

This book details the author's personal and professional experiences with and opinions about charitable giving. The author is not a licensed financial consultant.

The author and publisher are providing this book and its contents on an "as is" basis and make no representations or warranties of any kind with respect to this book or its contents. The author and publisher disclaim all such representations and warranties, including, for example, warranties of merchantability and financial advice for a particular purpose. In addition, the author and publisher do not represent or warrant that the information accessible via this book is accurate, complete, or current.

The statements made about products and services have not been evaluated by the U.S. government. Please consult with your own Certified Public Accountant or financial services professional regarding the suggestions and recommendations made in this book.

Except as specifically stated in this book, neither the author or publisher, nor any authors, contributors, or other representatives will be liable for damages arising out of or in connection with the use of this book. This is a comprehensive limitation of liability that applies to all damages of any kind, including (without limitation) compensatory; direct, indirect, or consequential damages; loss of data, income, or profit; loss of or damage to property and claims of third parties.

You understand that this book is not intended as a substitute for consultation with a licensed financial professional. Before you begin any financial program, or change your lifestyle in any way, you will consult a licensed financial professional to ensure that you are doing what's best for your financial condition.

This book provides content related to the topics of finances and economic living. As such, use of this book implies your acceptance of this disclaimer.

Table of Contents

Introduction:

You Can Be a Philanthropist – At Any Income Level

You are busy, generous by nature, and want to do good. You care about social justice and about preserving institutions important to you, your family, and your community. You want to solve pressing personal, family, neighborhood, or worldwide problems. You may be interested in working on behalf of a particular population, such as children or veterans or the disabled. Perhaps you feel a bit guilty that you can't do more. At the same time, you definitely want accountability for your charitable gifts of both dollars and time, and want to know their impact. And you likely now make most of your charitable donations in response to mail, social media, or direct personal requests.

For fifty years, I have volunteered for, been employed by, and consulted to dozens of nonprofit organizations in several sectors. I've built a practice advising individuals, couples, families, and business owners on organizing their charitable giving, as well as their homes and work lives. And I've taught many classes and workshops on philanthropy and fund raising. Among the many things I've learned is that most people would like more guidance when it comes to their giving.

If you are one of these people, **A POCKETFUL OF CHANGE** can help you increase the effectiveness of your gifts, and address the many common impediments to giving, by helping you:

- Define your giving goals,

- Identify giving opportunities in line with those goals,

- Evaluate charities' requests for contributions, and

- Ensure that your gifts do the most good for others and for you.

Charitable giving can be much more than simply responding to requests for donations from worthy causes. It can be a way for you to get your ideas heard, express your passions, be creative, and have fun. My personal mission is to help repair and improve the world by fostering thoughtful charitable giving. And while this may not be your mission, I hope you find that taking time to think about and organize your giving will bring you more meaning, satisfaction, and pleasure from the gifts you do make.

The New American Micro-Philanthropist

Have you ever participated in a charity bike-a-thon, supported a friend's new film release through GoFundMe, brought canned goods to the food pantry, served as a leader for your daughter's Girl Scout troop, or helped a local family in need via a Facebook appeal?

Then you are a philanthropist – which actually means "lover of mankind."

More than 75% of American households make a gift to one or more nonprofit organizations each year. In 2015, the average household gave $2,974,[1] hardly the huge amount most people connect with "philanthropic giving." Those who itemized deductions on their income tax return gave slightly more. During the past 50 years, the ratio of "individual-to-other sources" giving has been remarkably consistent: about 72% from living individuals and another 8% from bequests. To put it another way, about 80% of the $373.25 billion donated in the U.S. in

---

[1] The Center on Philanthropy at Indiana University.

2015[2] came not from foundations or corporations, but from individuals like you. And these numbers apply only to gifts made to the approximately 1.8 million IRS-registered nonprofit organizations. They are only part of the "wider world of giving," which can extend to supporting political candidates, trade organizations, or the family in your town whose home was just lost to a fire.

As you can see from these statistics, it's not just the rich who give. **A POCKETFUL OF CHANGE** is for those who may not have a lot to give, and who want to make the most effective use of their charitable dollars.

Throughout this book, you will see in italics direct quotes from my clients and students, people like you who would like to get more from what they give. Here's one:

I am continually surprised at how many people donate so much money without having a plan or a vision. I'm not sure they even understand how their gifts will be used, or whether their money is doing what they want it to do.

Beginning to Think Mindfully about Your Giving

By organizing your gifts, you **can** make a difference!

I just graduated, and am now earning enough to be able to do more than pay the rent. I don't have much to give, so I do want to make my gifts count.

Hearing and seeing all the groups that want me to contribute is extremely confusing and stressful. I don't know these people asking for money and I don't know how the money

---

[2] *Giving USA 2016: The Annual Report on Philanthropy for the Year 2015*, a publication of Giving USA Foundation, 2016, researched and written by the Indiana University Lilly Family School of Philanthropy.

really gets used. The idea of finally having an organized plan for how I am going to contribute, instead of just handing out dollars and hoping it is of some use, is a tremendous relief.

If your house is like mine, beginning each October, you begin to receive a surge in requests from many different worthy causes. How do you decide which, if any, to support, and at what level? How do you say "no" to causes you don't wish to or cannot support? Do you tend to give in response to a person, or to a cause? What factors might influence your giving?

As with other aspects of your life, especially your financial life, it is more efficient and more effective to have a goal and a plan, and to stick to it, while allowing some room for flexibility and spontaneity.

When you match your gifts with your goals, not only are you doing good, you also can get enormous satisfaction from doing so. Charitable giving can be a profoundly creative act, nurturing you as well as the recipients of your gifts.

That said, there is nothing wrong – and a lot right – with simply sending checks to one or more organizations whose appeals you get each fall. Potentially, though, there can be much more pleasure in initiating the gift – that is, when you are giving **proactively**, not reactively.

When you give your money and time, you have the freedom to try out new ideas, to do a project your way, without having to listen to those who tell you it can't be done.

To be sure that even your modest gifts have a major impact, you can create a Charitable Giving Plan, and then review it on a regular basis. How can you begin? Read on.

Part One:
Creating Your Charitable Giving Plan

Chapter One:
What Do You Want Your Gifts to Do for You?

Your Charitable Giving Plan is an organized system of what, why, how, to whom, and when you plan to give.

In its final form, it may be as simple as a series of notes, the results of the completed worksheets you will find in this book, and/or remembered conversations with your giving partner(s).

Or it may be a more formal outline, a diagram closely matching the wheel on the previous page, or a spreadsheet. Whatever form you use to express it, your Charitable Giving Plan will be as personal as your choices.

To begin, take a look at the wheel. It illustrates the six primary components that you may incorporate as you formulate your Charitable Giving Plan. Please note that thinking about each of these components is likely to inform and reshape your thinking about the others, so organizing your Charitable Giving Plan can feel a bit like doing a puzzle.

As an aid to those who are just beginning to consider creating a Charitable Giving Plan, I've numbered and organized the chapters into what many will find to be a useful sequence.

What do you want your gifts to do for you? This question may seem odd as a place to begin. However, human nature dictates that everyone wants something when they give, whether it is joy from helping others (which makes the donor feel better about him/herself) or the satisfaction of saving money on taxes (which also makes the donor feel pretty good).

A candid appraisal of what you want from your giving is essential as you begin to shape your Charitable Giving Plan. For instance, if your heart's desire is to be thought of as a philanthropist, or to be considered a "big donor" somewhere, then you probably would want to take two specific actions.

One would be to concentrate all or most of your allocated charitable dollars for the year into one large gift. The next would be to choose as the recipient a relatively small nonprofit organization, where a gift of that size would put you in the "inner circle" of donors.

For example, a gift of $3,000, while very handsome, is unlikely to yield a personal, handwritten letter of thanks from the president of an Ivy League university. However, it very well might get you an invitation to a major donor dinner at a community college or small private school.

If you own a small business, you might seek to increase your visibility, or to encourage employee loyalty, by offering a matching gift program.

Perhaps you crave the thrill of creating and implementing an exciting new community betterment project.

Or just maybe, you want the quiet satisfaction of knowing you truly have changed one life for the better.

"Know Thyself" said the Delphic Oracle, and this applies as well to knowing the type of giver you are. There are two kinds of charitable people: those who work to fight wrongdoing, and those who work to promote good. Once in a while, there is overlap, but most of us fall squarely into one category or the other. And both are absolutely necessary.

As you begin with #1 on the Creating Your Charitable Giving Plan wheel, some of the following ideas from other micro-philanthropists may help to inspire your thinking about what you want your gifts to do for you.

To gain satisfaction for doing good work.

The real estate firm I work for recently established a charitable foundation. All the agents are encouraged to give. We support the Epilepsy Foundation, Children's Hospital, the local breast cancer coalition, and a shelter for victims of domestic violence, among others. I feel proud to be part of a team that is doing so much for our community.

To earn "brownie points" with boss or family.

It doesn't hurt your career when you show up to support the boss's favorite charity. She even gives us three paid days off a year to volunteer for Habitat for Humanity. I brought my husband and we worked alongside my boss and her son, all of us in blue jeans – quite a change from the culture at the brokerage firm where we work!

To fulfill a religious obligation.

One of the five pillars of my faith, Islam, is zakat, *which means both "purification" and "growth." It is based on the principle that all things belong to God, and it is our job to take care of that wealth. What we own is purified by setting aside a portion for the needy. This cutting back encourages new growth, similar to pruning a plant. Each Muslim personally calculates his or her own zakat. Normally, it is about 2.5% of capital. In addition, we are taught to give as much as possible to* sadaqa, *roughly translated as "voluntary charity," preferably in secret.*

For tax advantages.

Let's be honest. Even do-gooder types give to charity in part to save from giving it to Uncle Sam. There are not many tax breaks left for us working stiffs.

To give back: "I've done well and now I want to do good."

I have always been proud that I'm a 'self-made man,' and have been known to boast about that fact once or twice. But my granddaughter has got me thinking about how I went all the way through public schools, used the public library for my studying, attended college on the G.I. bill, and got a start-up loan from the Small Business Administration back in its very first year. She points out that without the tax dollars of others, I might still be a poor farm boy from Mississippi, shoveling out the horse stalls, instead of owning the largest farm equipment retail store in three counties. So now I'm thinking about giving some of my hard-earned money to try to give a leg up to another scrappy farm kid – maybe a scholarship, maybe a loan to get him started in business.

To promote our business.

We want folks to think well of us in the community where our store is located, so we try to give to as many neighborhood causes as we can afford.

To express my personal philosophy: "I believe that our government should not be in the welfare business."

I don't give to organizations. I want to see results. So I give directly to people I know who are down on their luck. I figure once they get back on their feet, they can help someone else in turn. If everybody would help their neighbors like this, we wouldn't need all those government handouts. None of that socialist stuff for me.

To be looked up to as a leader in the community.

If I were to be perfectly honest, I would have to say that I choose where and how I give my time and my donations by how useful they are to the growth of my career. Rotary, Chamber of Commerce, the town Business Association, and any industry-related events get first claim on my time and my dollars. Since I've only been out of college for a couple of years, and I'm still new to the business world, I am watching closely how the "big shots" get ahead.

For personal gratification: it helps me feel good.

I get a great deal of satisfaction when I think about the twelve boys and girls from low-income families who got to go to school this year with new backpacks and supplies, thanks to the gift I made to the local "Smart Start" program. I like to think that I'm partly responsible for their academic success, even though I haven't set foot in a classroom in more than 10 years!

To assuage guilt.

I work in a large city. Every day I have to pass the homeless, sitting out on the sidewalk even in miserable weather. As I walk to my comfortable office, where I earn a comfortable living, I find that what I drop into their cups and buckets is increasingly large. I guess I feel guilty that I have so much and they do not.

To get recognition.

It is important to me as a woman to get recognition for my gifts. When you look at a building at a university or a new wing of the library, whose names do you see there? Men's. Sometimes women's — but those are almost always wives and mothers of the men who gave the money. I think women are too humble. We need to start to claim our power through our philanthropy — even if it's just getting named in the program for giving $25 to the high school drama club.

To honor or remember a friend, neighbor, colleague, or loved one.

For less than the cost of weekend at the beach community where my brother spent so much time, I was able to purchase a beautiful stone bench facing the ocean he loved so dearly. It gives me great comfort to see others enjoy the view and to read the inscription with his name.

To improve my own mental health.

When I first got involved with animal rescue work, I was recovering from a serious depression. Having a place to get up and go every day absolutely saved my life. Working to raise money for those poor abandoned pets gave me a reason to go on – a purpose larger than myself.

To be liked by peers and colleagues.

I buy candy bars for the school band uniform drive, holiday wrapping paper from my neighbor's kids for their youth group, daffodils to support the cancer society, and I guess I'm a sucker for every walk-a-thon and good cause that I'm asked to contribute to. I don't particularly need this stuff, but they seem like good causes, and I want to be thought of as a "team player" at work and a good neighbor at home.

To show my outrage.

Immediately after the 2016 presidential election, I felt so powerless, and like there was absolutely nothing I could do to change things. Then I saw on Facebook that lots of like-minded folks began giving very generously to organizations working for progressive causes. Someone even named these "Rage Donations." That expressed my mood perfectly, and I was happy to dig deeper than usual to show my support.

"Insurance."

I make a nice gift each year to the Medical Center. If they ever have to bring me in on a stretcher, I know they'll take good care of me!

To provide a current or future income stream with immediate tax benefits.

The Charitable Gift Annuity I set up with our local community foundation will continue to give me a fixed income each year for the rest of my life. When I pass on, they will use my gift to support the charities I have selected. Plus, I get a tax benefit now, and I avoided the capital gains tax because I donated securities.

To become involved with a community of like-minded individuals.

After my husband of 28 years left me for a woman just a bit older than our daughter, I found great comfort at a support group at the local women's center. I met strong, capable women – including many who had started over again in mid-life – who are working to put women into state and local office. Whether I'm helping to write the newsletter, lobbying at the State House, or raising money for candidates, I feel like my efforts really matter.

To get ahead socially or at work.

Let's face it. If you make the society pages because you are a big donor, people notice you. You have to go to the big events and then network, network, network. I never would have my current job if not for a connection I made through the Symphony.

To salve a pain.

The school department in our town just announced that it will be building two multi-stall, gender-neutral bathrooms at the high school, before the fall semester starts. I knew this would be a burden on the school budget, and that not all taxpayers would agree, so I quietly wrote a check. It's too late for me, but my hope is that even one transgender teen won't have to suffer the way I did.

To be competitive.

When they ask for gifts for our 25th college reunion, I know I won't be anywhere near the largest donor – hah! But I just want to be sure I give more than my old roommate – who always got the girl, the grades, everything I didn't have – and didn't hesitate to let me know it. Now that I'm doing well enough, I just want to see my name in a category above his on the class donor list!

To have my ideas both heard and given a forum.

I couldn't find any organization in our community doing the work most important to me: developing alternative methods of transportation. Here in our suburban town, everyone gets in their car, usually alone, drives to work or school, and drives home again. My dream is to work with others on creating a free bike system, on improving public transit, and on solar-powered mini-cars – anything other than energy-guzzling private automobiles. So I spent a little money and printed up some flyers and posted them around town. Then I set up a website and announced a meeting for other like-minded citizens. Wow, was I surprised! More than 50 people showed up at the first meeting. We're off to a great start!

To make a bequest when you have no heirs or do not wish to leave (all) assets to heirs.

Collecting antique toys has been my passion for most of my life. I can't imagine that any of my own children would be interested in preserving or expanding the collection; they would sell the whole kit and caboodle before I'm even cold in the ground. So I have arranged instead to will it to the local museum. That way, I can rest assured knowing my treasure is in good hands. Won't my children be surprised?

To leave a legacy.

My track coach made a big difference in my life. I wanted to give him something with meaning, something lasting. So we contacted the local community fund in the city where I went to high school and set up a donor-advised fund. From the interest, we are able to give a trophy and a $250 cash prize each year to the student who exemplifies the ideals taught by Coach Burke: sportsmanship, hard work, and team effort. And I get to attend the annual Awards Assembly and make the presentation – what a thrill!

Giving together as a couple unites us with a shared purpose.

My partner and I come from very different backgrounds, and were raised with very different philosophies of charitable giving. When we sit down together at the end of each month, and then again at the end of the year, to sort through all the requests and to decide how to allocate our charitable dollars, we always discover new things about each other. Through our decision-making process, we've learned patience, how to see the other's point of view, tolerance, how to compromise, and even how to find humor in the process. We do not support all the same causes, but there's enough overlap so that we can feel good about ourselves as a couple as well as individuals.

To be perceived by others as generous.

I've got an ego as big as a house. I like to think that in spite of this, I'm a pretty generous guy. But frankly, I feel much better when others know it too!

To teach my children and/or my grandchildren about giving.

We are not a wealthy family, but we think it is very important to involve our children in our philanthropy. On the first day of each month, we hold a family meeting and together decide how to allocate the $50 we set aside for charity monthly. The older children do research about local charitable organizations, and the younger two participate in saving their good used clothing and toys for needy children. Maybe it's just my imagination, but I really think my kids are a lot less spoiled and greedy than many of their friends.

Because it could be me.

Having been through what I consider to be about an average share of both joys and troubles, I am so grateful to have reached this stage of life with my health intact, a loving family, a supportive community, a roof over my head, and good food to eat. Every day I read the newspapers, and I see things that could just about break your heart: racial discrimination, families losing children to the dreadful opioid epidemic, industrial pollution ruining our rivers and even the air we breathe, not to mention the usual murder, mayhem, and political shenanigans going on. I feel very blessed that, at least for now, I am not suffering, at least not directly. So out of gratitude, I give to the causes that help fight these problems. It's never going to be enough, just one person, but if we all chip in to help, we can at least make a dent.

Your reasons for giving – be they altruistic, a bit self-interested, or, if you are like most donors, a combination of both – are yours (and your giving partners') alone. Understanding what it is you want personally from your gifts will help you as you begin to think about the causes and organizations that are important to you.

Consider:

What do you want your gifts to do for you? Can you identify your "giving personality?" Do you prefer to work for the good, or against the bad? Are you more inclined to work to create social change, or to support and strengthen existing organizations? What do you hope to get from your giving?

You may choose to record your answers to these and the questions following each chapter in a written "giving journal," on your tablet or computer, or in a note-taking app.

Chapter Two:
What Do You Want Your Gifts to Do for Others?

The second step in creating your Charitable Giving Plan will be to begin to define your giving interests: the causes, fields, and populations most important to you. At the same time, you also will be thinking about what it is you want your gifts to accomplish, that is, what you want your gifts to do for others.

The following worksheets will help you begin to define your giving interests and priorities. If you will be working with a giving partner (see Chapter Three), each of you can complete these worksheets, then compare notes.

WORKSHEET ONE:
WHY DO YOU GIVE?

List five organizations to which you gave either time or money in the past few years. Then note the reason you gave to each organization. For example: "my neighbor asked me to donate," "it's the charity my mother always supported," or "I believe in the cause." And if you can remember, also note how you first became involved with each organization or cause.

Organization   Reason(s) for giving   How got involved?

1.

2.

3.

4.

5.

What are some of the reasons you wrote in the middle column? What did you learn from completing this exercise? Do you see any similarities among your answers?

The next worksheet will help you think about ***why*** you give, and what activity or need might spark your interest. Of course, there are no "right" or "wrong" answers.

WORKSHEET TWO:
QUESTIONS TO CONSIDER AS YOU DEFINE YOUR GIVING INTERESTS:

What activities do you enjoy? Include those you share with your family, your partner, your colleagues, and your friends.

Might you wish to encourage, support, or promote any of these activities to a particular population, for example: children, immigrants, residents of your town, the elderly, the disabled, or students at your school or college?

There are many reasons why people make charitable gifts. Do you have a particular reason, or a philosophy of giving?

If you were asked to define "your community" what would you say it is? (Hint: it can be geographic, social, work-related, political, hobby-related, spiritual, economic, or a combination).

Again, take some time to reflect on your answers. If applicable, compare your reflections with those of your giving partner(s).

Did completing these exercises give you any more insight into your giving preferences? Others who've completed these exercises said:

For many years, I gave most of my donations to my alma mater. But I've since come to realize that colleges have resources that hungry people don't. If I'm going to give money and time, it's going to be for people who lack resources.

I've moved so many times in my life that I don't have any place that I'd really call "home" when it comes to geography. I think the colleagues in my field – who are spread out all over the globe – are the closest I come to community. And for certain, if I heard of one of them needing a hand, I'd be the first to donate.

How do I divide up my gift money? A little global, a little pretty, a little hungry, a little education, a little medical, a little Jewish.

Often, we give because we are asked. We give in response to a direct mail solicitation that touches our heart. We give when we hear of a disaster on the other side of the world – or in our own neighborhood.

But there is nothing shameful or wrong with getting pleasure from your gifts – even though you may be giving for the noblest of reasons. As you examine what you wrote in the worksheets above, compare the causes to which you gave to what you truly care about passionately. How would you really like your money to be put to use?

Sometimes, I think about what I would do if I won big in the lottery. For me, the answer is easy: I would give most of the money away. At this stage in my life, I really don't need anything. I'd like to endow a scholarship fund to help deserving young people get an education. That would be my goal.

The problem I see as most pressing is that so many of the homeless people in our city, and probably many other cities, are mentally ill. I know for sure that there are not enough beds for treatment, and that's just a shame. If I could change one thing, I would make sure that everyone who needed it had access to good-quality, compassionate, and affordable mental health care. In a country as wealthy as ours, no one should have to live on the streets because the health care system failed them.

Animal rights are very dear to my heart. I just don't understand how some people can breed animals for profit, then turn them loose. Those puppy mills have got to go. I would like to be sure that there are no-kill shelters for every domestic animal, and that they are taken care of properly until good, loving homes can be found for them.

I would support young artists just starting out, to help them launch their careers.

How can a person like me, who doesn't earn a lot, even begin to figure out to decide how to disperse my very few charitable dollars? I really, really want to make a difference – I just don't know how.

While certainly not comprehensive, the following list may give you a few ideas as you begin to decide which field or fields of interest you will support.

TWELVE FIELDS OF INTEREST FOR GIVING

Animals: Habitat, protection, rescue, research, shelter, welfare, zoo.

Arts: Arts education, dance, symphony, theater, visual; or direct support to an artist, dancer, or musician.

Culture: Media, museum, private library.

Education: Adult, college, learning disabilities, primary, secondary, vocational, S.T.E.M., or a specific field of study.

Environment: Alternative transportation, conservation, endangered species or habitats, plants, pollution control, recycling education, bodies of water.

Health: Addiction treatment, clinics, education, hospitals, mental health, nutrition, prevention, promotion, specific disease research or treatment.

Humanities: Exhibits, historical societies, performances, preservation, reenactments.

Human Services: Camps, crisis management, domestic violence survivors, food/nutrition, housing, legal services, job training, public safety, recreation, sports, welfare-to-work.

Political: Activism, candidates, civil society, human rights, international relations, peace, security.

Public service: Civil rights, police and firefighters, municipality, library, volunteerism, voter education.

Spiritual: Education, meditation, missionary, seminary, houses of worship, yoga, tai chi.

Technology: Classes in coding, web design, programming; incubators, start-ups.

Working With a Specific Population

If you find it challenging to define a particular population to which you are drawn, the list below may help as you think about how you want to direct your gifts. Which, if any, of these resonate with you?

TWENTY TARGET POPULATIONS FOR GIVING

Children
Community members (however you define "community")
Civic groups
Disabled
Displaced homemakers
Elderly
Ethnicity, race, or nationality
Families
Homeless
Immigrants/Refugees
Low-income
Members of a particular profession
Men and/or **Boys**
Minority or a **marginalized group**
People with a specific disease
Political candidates (tax restrictions apply)
Religious congregations (or a particular religion/order)
Students
Veterans
Women and/or **Girls**

Again, please note that this list is only a suggestion. You may have your own way of thinking of specific populations that are not mentioned here. Although it may feel like a challenge to choose from among all these worthy causes and populations, taking the time to do so will help make for more satisfying giving.

What Would You Most Like to Accomplish with Your Gifts?

Will it be to solve a problem or support an organization that has been important to you or to a family member? Do you want to help promote a cause? Assist a young or talented musician or artist? Help find a cure for a particular disease? Honor a friend or remember a loved one?

Is your main purpose in giving to help the needy or less fortunate? Is your goal to help make the world a more beautiful place? Or to fulfill a religious obligation? If you are not sure yet, here are a few more questions to guide you:

WORKSHEET THREE:
THINKING ABOUT WHAT YOU WANT YOUR GIFTS TO DO FOR OTHERS:

If you could change one thing about your community (however you define it), and had the power, resources, and time to do so, what would it be?

If you could change one thing about your country, and had the power, resources, and time to do so, what would it be?

What is the best way to go about creating that change?

What one small first step can you take towards creating that change?

What would you spend your energy or dollars on preserving or enhancing?

What would you most like to have accomplished before you leave the earth?

What Would You Like Your Gifts to Do for Others?

Here are some reasons gathered from clients, students, and workshop participants, which may inspire you as you think about what you want your gifts to do for others.

To create social change.

I want to see to it that no child goes to bed hungry. We have enough resources to feed all our nation's children. Last year, I helped to start an organization to raise awareness about children and hunger, and most of our efforts now go to public education. We work with food pantries and churches, and speak in communities all over the state. Soon, we'll be all over the country!

To maintain the status quo.

My wife and I met in college. We are both very active in the Alumni Association, and take pride in the excellence and fine reputation of our alma mater. In addition, each year we make a modest gift to the college scholarship fund, in order to attract the same high-caliber students we fancy ourselves to have been.

To help repair my corner of the world.

I care deeply about the environment. I can't really do much by myself about global warming or air pollution except to lobby. But when our city fathers decided to treat our town's pond with chemicals to get rid of pervasive weed growth, I organized and helped to finance an educational program to teach residents how to prevent and eliminate weed growth naturally. It took a little longer, but I am really pleased with the results of our combined efforts. We can even swim there again.

To help beautify the world.

I am proud that my great-grandparents were among the founders of the Denver Art Museum, and I continue to support it with gifts of time and money. I am considering making a gift of my great-grandmother's small personal art collection, but so far, I am not ready to part with it. Perhaps I will leave it to the Museum in my will.

To help address a particular problem.

I'm working on getting some books into an inner-city school. I was visiting the school where a friend works and was shocked to see a virtually empty library. My friend explained that teachers bought their own books but were then reluctant to let students take them home, as they couldn't afford to replace them. The solution seemed so obvious to me. I'm surrounded by friends who have more books than space to shelve them. I see yard sales with books for a quarter, and live in a town with three used-book stores. This is something that I can do. And I hope it will just grow and grow.

To repay charity or kindness given to me earlier in my life.

Having been on the receiving end of charity, I have a new respect for giving. Receiving an anonymous gift of $5,000 very literally saved my life. It was so unexpected! It acted as a jolt – jarring me out of years of an entangled mess of bad luck, bad health, bad decisions. It gave me hope – something I had no reason to have anymore. And it gave me the very real tool of financial support to dig myself out of a terrible situation. So now I try not to let a day go by where I haven't at the very least noticed where I can be of help.

To respond to a disaster.

The recent hurricane made me realize just how blessed we are simply to have a roof over our heads. My kids and I worked together, collecting blankets and warm clothes to bring to the high school gym, where those who lost their homes were being sheltered.

To promote a particular cause or philosophy.

Our family cares deeply for animals, and 100% of our charitable gifts go to support animal rights, animal welfare, and vegetarianism.

Because we cannot always know the whole story.

I give money to people who ask me for it. This is very unpopular with most and it is a private decision I have made. I know a lot of people fret over whether the money given is really helpful. A friend told me a story 20 years ago that settled my mind on this issue. He was 18 and in his first year of college. He received a phone call one morning from his dad letting him know that his grandmother had unexpectedly died the night before. My friend was shaken and ran out of the house without his wallet. When he got to the subway station and realized that he had no change, he began asking for help. People ignored him, and he was deeply upset that no one would help him get on the subway. I think of him being only 18 and needing desperately to get home. People generally don't ask for money because it is a fun thing to do.

As this last example shows, sometimes a gift of just one subway token can have an influence on someone's life.

Your reasons for giving may be yours alone, or you may share them with someone close to you. The next chapter talks about giving together with others.

Consider:

What do you want your gifts to do for others? What would you most like to accomplish with your gifts? Which fields, areas of interest, and populations do you want to support? If there are too many, what criteria will you use to narrow your choices?

Chapter Three:
Who Will Be Involved in Creating Your Plan?

While each of us has our own preferences, ideas, and loyalties when it comes to charitable giving, many of us will, at some time, make some or all of our gifts collaboratively with others: your "giving partner(s)".

Your giving partner could be your spouse or life partner, children or grandchildren; your siblings, parents, or other family members; or members of your Giving Circle (see below). You might participate in a crowd-funding charitable appeal, giving with thousands of others you'll never meet. If you're a business owner (see Chapter Nine), you may involve your partner, investors, vendors, employees, or customers in your giving. You also might choose to work with a professional organizer, life coach, or friend to help you define and decide on your giving goals.

Depending on your reasons for giving, your own tax situation, and the dollar amounts you plan to donate, you also may include financial professionals, such as your attorney, banker, licensed financial planner, insurance agent, or investment counselor, in creating your plan.

The thought expressed above by the late Paul Ylvisaker, with whom I had the great privilege and honor to study philanthropy many years ago, points out that while it's not always easy to give in collaboration with others, especially family, the results can be positive, even life-changing.

How can you work with others to be sure that both your desires – and those of your giving partner(s) – are addressed?

Giving As a Couple

Giving as a couple – that is, taking time to talk about what means the most to each of you, as well as you two together – can add an entirely new dimension to your relationship. If you will be giving with a spouse or life partner, how you approach charitable giving will be part of a much larger discussion about money, values, and how you negotiate differences.

Long ago, when we were first married, my partner made a large donation each year to his alma mater. Now, I had no problem with that, since I had my own preferred charities. However, when the university routinely sent mailings and event invitations only to him, not me, I felt slighted. We discussed him making the gift in both our names, so I would be included. But as we talked, he realized that he might like to redirect some of that annual gift to a cause that we both care about. So it wasn't an "either/or" situation, just a reallocation of some of his charitable resources.

My wife, bless her heart, is such a soft touch. She gives something to everyone who asks. And it seems like the more she gives, the more mailing lists she gets added to. We had to sit down – and using the tools we gained in Gail's class – to figure out what was most important to both of us.

In recognition of the skills, support, and values he gained as a Boy Scout, my husband always gave to national BSA. A few years back, before they reversed their decision to allow openly gay Troop leaders, I was incensed at their exclusionary policy. My husband, who is an Eagle Scout, did not feel as strongly as did I that we should not be supporting the organization at all. After many heated discussions, we decided to reallocate our giving away from National and to the local Council, and to restrict our gift to camperships. Four underprivileged boys get to go to Scout Camp for two weeks each year, and I'm good with that.

Talking with your spouse or partner about how you will make your charitable gifts can bring up a lot of deep-seated issues in your relationship, as money often reflects power and control and who's in charge. How and to whom you make your gifts can express love, appreciation, and generosity – or anger and resentment.

This is tough to talk about, but when I discovered that my (now ex-) husband was having an affair – well, the betrayal, shock, and hurt was bad enough, but then I thought about how he was also risking my health and my life! I took his AmEx Platinum card (the one I "wasn't allowed" to use) and made a substantial donation to the local AIDS Coalition. He paid the bill and never said a word.

My partner and I met on Thanksgiving. We'd both volunteered to serve dinner at Rosie's Place (a Boston shelter and support center for poor and homeless women) since we were each single, far away from our families, and couldn't afford to travel home. So you could say that giving is at the core of our relationship. Now that we've been blessed with two beautiful daughters who are old enough to help, serving Thanksgiving dinner at Rosie's is an annual tradition. As the start to the holiday season, our service is fundamental to our family life and sets the tone for a meaningful Christmas.

Giving As a Family

If you will be giving as a family, that is, with your spouse and/or children, it's often a good idea to start the process by creating a family giving mission statement. It is an idealistic, concise statement of what your family hopes to accomplish with its giving.

A mission statement expresses both your purpose and your values. What is your aim, and by what principles will you operate? Even if you cannot come to a final agreement on what your mission should be, the conversations you have about your goals, and what each of you wants, can be valuable in and of themselves.

We decided that our top priority was to address child hunger – or what we later found out is now called "food insufficiency." Our children were especially troubled to realize that kids their own age – as close as in the next town over! – sometimes went to bed hungry, or had to get subsidized lunches at school because their families couldn't afford to pay for them. So after much discussion, we came up with this simple statement: "We are committed to helping to solve the problem of hungry children, especially in our local community."

If you have children, they are observing you all the time – to see if what you say is consistent with what you do, and how you spend, save, and donate your time and dollars.

Involving your children in your volunteer work and other charitable activities can set an example for a lifetime of giving, one that they someday may pass along to their own children.

We offer our children a "giving allowance" in addition to their regular spending money for lunch and stuff they want to buy. Once they save up, we discuss who and what they care to help and why.

When giving with children, it's also crucial to listen. You may learn something.

My preteen daughter began to set aside some of her babysitting money to sponsor a child in Africa through Save the Children. This wasn't something I suggested to her – I think she saw an ad on TV or in a magazine. When I asked her why she was doing this, she just said, "Mom. We have so much."

It was my son's turn to pick a charity with our monthly allotment. He chose the Rock & Roll Hall of Fame. OK, not my first choice. But he was so proud, and he loved that he could tell his friends that he was a donor when they saw his members-only tee shirt.

Working together as a family – whether volunteering at the local animal shelter, or holding monthly family meetings to decide how to donate a portion of your income (or children's allowances), is a great way to spend good quality family time together.

Involving children or grandchildren in charitable giving can be a powerful way to try to transmit our own values, and to learn more about theirs.

We want to make sure our young children grow up learning how to give to others and to save, rather than demanding every darn thing they see on TV. So we volunteer together at clean-up drives, collecting Toys for Tots, and library books for the Young Literacy program. When we shop at the grocery store, we always add an item or two for our community's food pantry.

What is the most important thing I can pass along to my grandchildren? It's not my money, that's for sure. I want them to learn kindness, to help others, to find purpose and meaning in their lives. Of course, wealth can provide a level of comfort, but at what cost to the quality of their spiritual well-being?

When the school Athletic Director in our small town was fired suddenly and unfairly for blowing the whistle on some shady practices by the coaching staff, he was left both without a job and with growing legal expenses. Outraged folks took up a donation and brought him three huge baskets full of staples and gift cards at Christmas – just enough to help out and to let him know that we support him and his efforts. Our daughter, who was very upset by the firing, made a gift of her own from her own earnings. She told me later it helped her feel less powerless, and like she was doing something to right the wrong that had been done.

Sometimes, we may not even think we're teaching our children about giving, but they're watching us. One divorced mother explains:

My 17-year-old son confessed to me one night that he was doing something odd. He told his father that he was taking a night class at the college extension program. Instead, he was going to a shelter to cook for the homeless. College guys were teaching him how to cook and part of the deal was that he then had to sit down and eat with the "clients." He was baffled by how happy this weekly event made him, and was sure that his success-oriented father just wouldn't understand.

Giving doesn't always work out the way you plan, but there are lessons to be learned from less-than-successful attempts too.

One day, when our daughter Olivia was 12, the temperature here in San Francisco was nearly a hundred and, as you may know, very few workplaces have air conditioning. We live on a steep hill, and see people slogging their way up from downtown, starting at about 4 pm. People looked miserable and Olivia decided to do something. She picked lemons from our lemon tree and made about 5 gallons of lemonade, baked a few dozen sugar cookies and set up a bridge table on our busy corner. She put up a sign that said, "Free lemonade and cookies."

What followed was a real stunner. A lot of people came over, and questioned Olivia mercilessly about what the "catch" was. Some took her at her word that she just thought people might like some lemonade and cookies, some actually changed direction so they wouldn't even have to walk near her lemonade stand. But for the people who stopped by, there was cold homemade lemonade, fresh cookies, and, more refreshing than that, actual conversation with others. This may be the only time anyone involved, my daughter included, will ever operate without any motive other than just seeing how a place (or a street corner) could be improved, where people might find the generous gesture just for the sake of doing it.

Giving with Your Extended Family

Giving together with your siblings, cousins, or other family members can create a special bond, especially if you do not live proximate to one another. Talking about your common goals and how you want to address them as a family can be an enriching experience for all.

We have a Cousins' Club – there are 24 of us all together, many of us very close. Rather than exchanging holiday gifts, we decided that we'd each put into a kitty $100, or whatever we can afford that year. Sometimes it's a bit more, sometimes less, no one keeps score. Then we make one group gift to a charity we take turns selecting. We divided ourselves into teams of six – so everyone gets a chance to choose once every four years. And every cousin gets one veto every year – so if the team chooses an organization one of us feels they just cannot support, he or she say can say "no" and the team tries again. But in more than 30 years now, that's happened only once. Sure, they've picked a few things I wouldn't necessarily support, but I'm OK with my cousins' choices.

When my sister's daughter successfully completed treatment for a rare form of childhood cancer, my older brother organized the whole extended family – our parents, five siblings and their children, cousins, aunts, and uncles, and our last living grandparent. We each chipped in what we were able to give, and together, we made a substantial family gift to the medical center that gave such good care to our beloved Hayley.

And my own family's giving story:

When our mother turned 70, we tried to think of a very special gift for her birthday. Because she has been a lifelong volunteer – starting with raising money for polio research, then for cancer research, and at the same time, serving as a Girl Scout leader and troop consultant, as well as UNICEF chair in the small town where she and our dad still live, the idea came to us to honor this commitment. We created the Arline Shapiro Community Service Award at the local high school, which is given each year to the student who "best embodies the spirit of volunteerism and community service." All the siblings chip in, and each winner gets a small cash prize, and his or her name is engraved on a permanent plaque, which hangs in a case next to all the athletic trophies. This past June, we made our 20th annual Award, which greatly pleased our mother. And her eldest grandson has pledged to organize all the cousins to continue the Award for another generation.

When you are giving with a spouse, partner, or other family members, leave some room for negotiation, so that your reason or reasons for giving can align, either wholly or in part, with theirs. You also may decide to give with a group of friends – or even strangers – and in that case, flexibility is one key to success.

Joining or Creating a Giving Circle

A Giving Circle is a group of friends, acquaintances, congregants, neighbors, or just like-minded individuals who pool their donations and together, research and decide how to select beneficiaries of their group grants. Giving circles offer social networking, peer-to-peer support, leadership opportunities, and peer education.

Often administered via the local Community Foundation (see Chapter Six), giving circles, a form of "grassroots micro-philanthropy" (see Chapter Ten), encourage collaboration with those who may not share all your political or religious views, or cultural or economic background. They tend to attract people who want to be more actively involved in philanthropy than just making a donation. In the U.S., about two-thirds of giving circle members are women, and members of minority groups and younger people make up a large percent of those involved.

According to a 2014 report by Jumpstart Labs, which surveyed 4,900 American households,[3] "one in eight donors makes a contribution through a giving circle, [and] nearly 40 percent of all giving-circle donors are under 40."

There is a list of current giving circles at this website: www.givingcircles.org. The examples below, drawn from that website, offer a small sample of the wide range and various priorities of different giving circles. It is not meant as an endorsement of any particular group – always do your own due diligence before joining or donating to a giving circle!

Dining for Women is a "global giving circle dedicated to transforming lives and eradicating poverty among women and girls in the developing world. Through member education and engagement, as well as the power of collective giving, Dining for Women funds grassroots organizations that empower women and girls and promote gender equity."

Cherry Blossom Giving Circle is "a group of volunteers committed to creating positive change in the Asian American and Pacific Islander (AAPI) communities of the Washington, DC metro area. Representing diverse cultures, professional backgrounds, perspectives, and interests, we have pooled our resources to support AAPI-serving nonprofits in the area. We

---

[3] Held, Tom. "Giving Circles Popular With Minorities and Younger Donors, Says Study," *Chronicle of Philanthropy*, July 3, 2014.

promote positive change in the area's underserved AAPI communities."

The San Francisco-based **Full Circle Fund** is "an active network of professionals who leverage their time, talent and connections to help nonprofit organizations launch new initiatives, make a greater impact and accelerate positive change in our community. We're made up of incredibly passionate, motivated and talented people who want to play a more active role in making the world a better place. What we do goes beyond simply writing a check, attending a fundraiser or volunteering for a day. Our members come together to think, learn and work hand-in-hand to affect change where it matters most."

For those who want to give internationally, global giving circles have a wider scope than your local community. Online or virtual giving circles serve those who cannot or don't wish to meet in person.

There are many resources on the internet that outline how to create or join an existing Giving Circle, and what you need to know as you proceed.

We give collectively to causes that we're passionate about. I love meeting with this group of like-minded women. The time we spend in researching each charity has brought me a level of knowledge about our community I never could have gained on my own. I've seen first-hand the issues my neighbors struggle with, as well as the amazing accomplishments they have achieved.

The first step in making thoughtful gifts with like-minded others – whether your partner, family, friends, or strangers – is to begin a continuing open and respectful discussion. Listening actively while advocating for your own preferences sometimes can be a challenge. Fortunately, many people find that the process of negotiation – which isn't always easy or painless – and having to reach consensus, not only helps bring their own priorities into sharper focus, but also broadens their giving outlook. Working on giving together with a partner or partners can be tremendously satisfying for all concerned.

Consider:

Who will be involved with creating and implementing your charitable giving plan? Which of your financial advisors, if any, might you call on to help implement your plan? How will you begin the discussion with your giving partner(s) about each of your priorities and goals? How will you resolve any conflicts?

Chapter Four:
What and How Much Will You Give?

There are many stories of ordinary folks who lived frugally, saved and invested wisely, and gave away a fortune late in life or via their estate.

Oseola McCarty, born in Mississippi in 1908, worked hard all her life. There were few opportunities for this African-American woman, who quit school after the sixth grade to care for her ailing aunt. She washed and ironed clothes, lived alone in a small house, and saved every nickel she did not absolutely have to spend. In 1995, she astounded the University of Southern Mississippi with her gift of $150,000. "I want to help somebody's child go to college," she said, in a statement released by the University (June 26, 1995). "I just want it to go to someone who will appreciate it and learn. I'm old and I'm not going to live always." The endowed Oseola McCarty Scholarship now helps "deserving African-American students with financial need."

In the winter of 2015, officials at the Brattleboro, Vermont public library and local hospital were shocked to receive bequests totaling $6 million from the recently deceased 92-year-old Ronald Read, a frugal New Englander who worked as a janitor and gas station attendant, and who apparently had a knack for the stock market. He also made a number of smaller gifts of money and property to other local charities.

Thomas Drey, a retired public school teacher, built his savings and a small inheritance from his father into a fortune by studying the stock market at the business branch of the Boston Public Library, and using what he learned there. When he died in 1997, the city received Mr. Drey's entire estate of $6.8 million, in gratitude for the use of its resources during his life.

Gilmore and Golda Reynolds of Osgood, Indiana lived simply all their lives, for many of those years in a one-bath, two-story home in a commercially zoned district. Investing their savings both in the stock market and in a few business ventures that paid off handsomely, much to the surprise of town officials and their neighbors, in 1999 they left $23 million to their town, population 1,800.

But you don't have to save and give millions like this to make a difference.

As create your Charitable Giving Plan, you may find that deciding how much to give will be determined in part by what you want your gifts to do – both for others and for you. Other factors may include:

- Your perception of your ability to give.
- What you learned about giving while growing up.
- What your religious, spiritual, or philosophical tradition (if any) teaches about giving.
- What you currently practice from your own tradition (if any).
- Whether or not you are asked personally to give.
- Your perception of how your gifts will be used, or cash donations spent.

Let's look at these one at a time.

Your Perception of Your Ability to Give

How much to give is a very personal decision. It depends on your goals and values, your current financial situation, and on how you feel about giving right now. Did you just go through a job loss or a divorce, and perhaps are more careful with money than usual? Did you just receive an inheritance or a large bonus, and so are able to be more confident about giving?

Your decision also may be based on how much volunteer time you give during the year. If your work, family, or other obligations keep you too busy to donate much time, you may choose to give more dollars. If you are a student or if you are retired, the opposite may be true.

How much you give also may depend on your perception of where you stand relative to others. These statistics, from the 2014 U.S. Bureau of the Census, will give you an idea.

WHERE DOES YOUR HOUSEHOLD STAND ON THE NATION'S ECONOMIC SCALE?[4]

If your household income is:	You're in the bottom:	You're in the top:
$ 8,600	5%	
$ 13,500	10%	
$ 22,500	20%	
$ 26,500	25%	
$ 34,000	33%	
$ 56,516		**50%**
$ 76,000		33%
$ 93,000		25%
$ 106,000		20%
$ 145,000		10%
$ 207,000		5%
$ 250,000		3%
$ 310,000		2%
$ 430,000		1%

Of all households in the U.S.

U.S. Bureau of the Census, 2014

Since the government currently subsidizes charitable giving through an income tax deduction for those not taking the standard deduction, the cost of your gift is reduced by your tax bracket.

For example, if you are single and earn up to about $38,000 in taxable income, you would be in the 15% tax bracket, and your gift of $100 would cost you only $85 (assuming you would have paid the other $15 to Uncle Sam by not claiming the charitable deduction). If you are in the 25% bracket (in 2017, taxable

---

[4] In 2015, the U.S. median income rose 5.2% from 2014 to $56,516, so that exact number has been inserted at the 50% mark on this chart.

income of about \$38,000-\$92,000), your \$100 gift would cost you just \$75, and so on.

What You Learned about Giving while Growing Up

What you give also depends in part on the messages about giving – both spoken and unspoken – you heard in your own home, as well as peer and community influences, while you were growing up.

What did you hear while growing up about giving?

I remember being taken by my parents to a fundraiser when I was a youngster. One fellow stood up at the after-dinner auction, and bid quite a lot "in honor of my Aunt Bess." Then another guy stood right up and said, "I'll bid [more] in memory of my beloved grandmother." As young as I was, I wondered why they were so competitive about something that was supposed to be for a good cause.

I learned that making money – and keeping it for oneself – was way more important than social justice. I had a lot to unlearn, and that's why I took this class.

I learned that it was good to make a lot of money, to be able to help others. But in order to help others, I first had to be financially secure myself.

My brothers and I heard: "you should always be generous to those less fortunate than you." But no one ever talked about the enormous pleasure we could get from giving. It's like feeling good or benefitting in any way from it was shameful or wrong.

I don't think I ever heard my parents talk about giving at all.

What Your Religious, Spiritual, or Philosophical Tradition (if any) Teaches about Giving

Nearly every religion, and many philosophical traditions, count charitable giving as one of their tenants. Through holy scriptures, prophets, spiritual and secular leaders, and philosophers, we are encouraged, urged, or commanded to help the poor and the needy, widows and orphans, and to help others get started in a business, so they not only can fend for themselves, but can then, in turn, give to others.

And when ye reap the harvest of your land, thou shalt not wholly reap the corners of thy field, neither shalt thou gather the gleanings of thy harvest. And thou shalt not glean thy vineyard, neither shalt thou gather every grape of thy vineyard; thou shalt leave them for the poor and stranger: I am the Lord your God. (Leviticus 19: 9-10)

They will question you concerning what they should bestow voluntarily. Say: 'Whatever good thing you bestow is for parents and kinsmen, orphans, the needy and strangers and whatever good you do God has knowledge of it.' (Koran 2: 215)

The Levels of Tzedakah:
Enabling the recipient to become self-reliant.
Giving when neither party knows the other's identity.
Giving when one knows the recipient's identity, but the recipient doesn't know the donor's identity.
Giving when one does not know the recipient's identity, but the recipient knows the identity of the donor.
Giving before being asked.
Giving after being asked.
Giving less than one should, but giving it cheerfully.
Giving begrudgingly. (Moses Maimonides, Mishnah Torah, Laws of Charity)

A place in God's court can only be attained if we do service to others in this world. (Guru Granth Sahib 26)

And now abideth faith, hope, charity, these three; but the greatest of these is charity. (I Corinthians 13:13)

Do good with what thou hast, or it will do thee no good. (William Penn)

A man's true wealth hereafter is the good he does in this world to his fellow man. (Moliere [Jean-Baptiste Poquelin])

Charity never humiliated him who profited from it, nor ever bound him by the chains of gratitude, since it was not to him but to God that the gift was made. (Antoine de Saint-Exupery)

The proper aim of giving is to put the recipient in a state where he no longer needs our gift. (C. S. Lewis)

What You Currently Practice from Your Own Tradition (if any)

As far back as I can remember, my family always has tithed, giving ten percent of income to charity. Giving the first ten percent not only is required by my Church, but it feels good. It's very empowering and very practical.

Consider giving as a regular part of your fiscal and spiritual practice. I find it fascinating to see the similarities among most religious teachings when it comes to giving.

It's very important to give generously, especially when you're scared about not having enough.

Why give? Because the Bible commands us to do so.

I appreciate that in the phrase, "cash flow," the emphasis is on the word "flow." If you hoard money, you end up only with the money you hoard. If you spend, give away, invest, or otherwise use your money, you keep it in circulation, and it comes back to you in a positive way.

Whether or Not You Are Asked Personally to Give

Those who are asked to give by a friend, relative, co-worker, or neighbor, not only are more likely to give, but to give more, than if they are approached by a phone call, email, or letter.

I'm a sucker for anybody who asks for a donation – especially if I do business with or play golf with the guy.

However, there is a significant gender difference. Contrary to what one might think, research shows that men are more likely to give to people; women to causes. That is, a man will respond to a personal "ask" because of the relationship, while a woman would be less likely to do so, unless she believes in the organization or cause.

Women, as a rule, don't necessarily respond to peer pressure around giving. While men often give because their friend or colleague asked them, women generally are more interested in building a relationship with an organization.

Tell me why the organization merits my time and dollars, and if this information resonates with my values and needs, I'm more likely to give.

I am not likely to respond positively to even a close friend who says, "I gave $100 to this cause. Why don't you match it?" I want to know more about the cause, and about what difference my gift can make to the institution or those it serves.

Your Perception of How Your Gifts Will be Used, or Cash Donations Spent

I've read that most people who give less than they could, do so not because they feel strapped for cash. Instead, they're concerned about how their gift will be used. Is the charity really on the up-and-up? Will their donation be used wisely? How can you tell?

The most common reason people do not give to charity is not because they lack (or think they lack) the funds to do so. Most often, people who do not give do not do so because they are unsure of how their donations will be used.

Those organizations and causes which are the most transparent should be the best positioned to receive gifts. However, there still is a lot of misunderstanding. One cannot always judge an organization's worthiness based strictly on the ratio of funds spent on administration to programs/services.

A brand-new nonprofit might spend close to 100% of its funds on administration in the first year, and that's to be expected. How else would they get started? They have to rent an office before they can see clients there. They need to pay for the lights, internet, and some basic furniture before they can serve the public.

Chapter Seven will give you more specific information on how to evaluate a charity before you make a donation.

What Will You Give?

Do you have more time, more money, or more goods? Who can use what you have to give? If your gift is unusual, or may require special care, is the charity prepared to receive it?

When I worked for a small human services organization, a potential donor (probably seeking a tax write-off) offered to give us a horse. No stall, no food, no way to transport it, no place to keep it. Just the horse. We had to decline the gift.

The amount you give, and the form it will take, largely will depend on two factors other than how much is available: your reason(s) for giving, and to whom you will make the gift, which is component #5 on the giving wheel.

For example, as you learned in Chapter One, if you have earmarked $3,000 to give to charity this year, and your primary reason for giving is to be thought of as a generous donor in your community, you might consider taking the entire amount and giving it to the smallest nonprofit in your area of interest. Three thousand dollars is a huge gift to many charitable organizations.

However, if your reasons for giving are to be able to respond to a disaster, and to promote a particular cause, you may choose to make a gift to that cause, and then set aside the rest of your funds to be able to respond quickly in the case of local, national, or international need.

You also may have a number of organizations in many different fields that appeal to you, and so you might make gifts of $25, $50, or more to each during the year.

Perhaps you don't have $3,000 – or even $300 – to donate, but you do want to be charitable. Your options for giving are many. In addition to **money** (cash, a pledge, or some of your securities or other assets); you can give **time** (your expertise, professional service, or hands-on help); or **goods** (used clothing or household items, artwork to a museum or photographs to a historical society, or a perhaps a family heirloom you don't wish to pass on to the next generation).

I don't have much to give. But then a friend told me about Dress for Success, a national nonprofit that helps a low-income woman enter into the workforce by giving her one good suit when she has an interview and another when she gets the job. Now, finally, here was something I could do. I now send at least two suits each season. They are still in style, and in good shape, and I am delighted to help.

If you do choose to give money, will it be:
- a predetermined percentage of your income (and if so, net or gross?),
- a fixed amount, or
- whatever is left over after all your other obligations are met?
- Or, will you give a portion of your assets?

Those who give through an automatic plan, such as payroll deductions, give at a higher rate than those who give "when the spirit moves them."

We determined that we could afford to give away $1000 last year. Some of it was earmarked for "on-the-spot" gifts: a family member needing a little help, or a co-worker doing a charity walk. The rest was divided among the four charities we have loyally supported for years.

At the end of the month, I divide whatever money I have left into two parts: one I save, and the other I give away. Some months it is more, some less. But I always give at least $10 a month, even if I come out short. I feel it's my obligation.

Staples like beans, pasta, and soup often are on sale at the grocery store. When boxes of spaghetti or bags of rice are 10 for $10, or tuna is 4 for $3.99, we buy an extra unit. We save these items until we fill a grocery bag, and then deliver it to our local food pantry.

There is a young mother of twins in our town, whose husband just walked out on her. I knew times would be tough and she wouldn't have much money for non-essentials. I also suspected that she wouldn't take a hand-out. So I purchased a gift certificate for the local toy store, and another one for the pizza shop, and mailed them to her anonymously with a note that read: 'Best wishes from a neighbor who cares'. I'm sure I got at least my money's worth of enjoyment imagining her face when she opened that envelope!

My nephew's school band entered a nationwide competition to be held on the west coast, and all the kids were supposed to raise funds for their travel expenses. He asked me to donate, and I felt bad that I was short on cash. But then I remembered all those airline miles I'd been saving for years – and was able to get him and his two best friends round-trip plane tickets!

My grandmother left me her elegant grand piano – a very lovely instrument, but one which I really have no room for in my tiny apartment. I was able to donate it to the professional musical theater group in the city next to the town where she lived. They were thrilled, and sent over professional piano movers to pick it up. It gives me a lot of pleasure to know that, rather than collecting dust here, it will be appreciated and used regularly.

Whether you have $5000 or $5 to donate this year, thoughtfully creating your Charitable Giving Plan will help you make most of your charitable donations. How will you choose the recipients of your gifts? Read on.

Consider:

What are you able to give: time, money, property, or a combination? How much will you give, and what timetable for giving will you use?

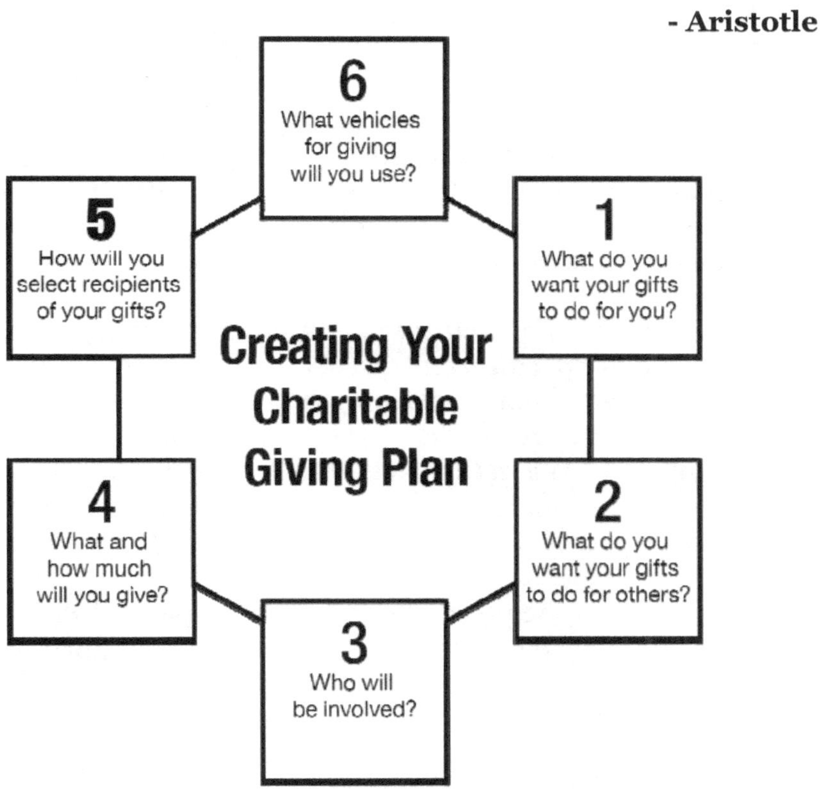

Chapter Five:
How Will You Select Recipients of Your Gifts?

Once you have identified your most important reason or reasons for giving, and have an approximate idea of how much you can set aside for giving, the next step is to choose the recipient(s) of your gifts, from among many worthwhile causes.

While the IRS has granted tax-exempt status to more than a million organizations, it can be argued that not all of them are "charities." It is estimated that only about one-quarter of nonprofits registered with the IRS actually do philanthropic work. The rest, says George McCully, president and CEO of the Massachusetts Catalogue for Philanthropy, "include things like condo associations, real estate trusts, trade associations, social clubs, cemeteries, teacher retirement funds, and so on."[5] While they are organized for the public good, they probably are not likely potential recipients for your gifts. But that leaves you with several hundred thousand organizations from which to choose – still an enormous number.

You are bombarded with all those charity ads on TV showing starving children, diseases, and abused animals, but you don't really know anything about these organizations or how they work. And then you look around in your own community and see actual need right in front of your eyes. It's hard not to just shrug and give up, especially when you don't have a lot to give. It's all just so overwhelming!

How will you begin to choose your recipients? Refer back to Worksheet One. The charities you have been supporting may be the ones you will continue to support, or, having read this far, you may decide to redirect some or all of your gifts.

We have always supported my dad's alma mater. But it has a huge endowment, and we would rather give our money to a smaller, local organization. Can you help us find a good match for our interests?

Each year I give to the Salvation Army, because, well, I've always given to them. They do good work. But this year, I'd like

---

[5] George McCully, Good-Bye, 'Nonprofit(s)'; Hello, 'Philanthropy'(-ies) and 'Charity'(-ies). PhilanTopic, a blog of opinion and commentary, Philanthropy News Digest, Foundation Center, October 29, 2016.

to find an organization more in line with my goals and I'm not sure how to start looking.

One principle of giving which I always share with my clients and students who feel overwhelmed is this: the smaller the community to which you belong, the more valuable your gifts. That is, only a finite amount of donors – usually a subset of members – are likely to give to your food co-op, your specific religious congregation, or to your community's senior center. At the same time, thousands or even millions of dollars will be donated to an international relief fund, religious federation, or national disease-specific organization.

And while many of these larger-scale, much more prominent efforts are vitally important, your small gift will have a larger impact when directed to a smaller, more local cause. You may find this principle to be helpful as you think about your giving.

Now refer back to Worksheet Two, in which you were asked to define "your community," noting that it can be geographic, social, work-related, political, hobby-related, spiritual, economic, or a combination. Or to think of it another way, to which organizations do you currently belong? In which are you active? Are there organizations to which you used to belong or to which you currently belong but are not active, including those in which you were active as a child or youth? For which do you feel the most affinity? What other memberships/affiliations (religious, political, social, occupational, etc.) do you hold that have meaning for you?

Now, consider each organization or community you listed. What might be the specific needs of that organization? Can you think of a way to make a gift of dollars, time, or goods that will benefit that community?

I am a proud member of my sorority, and each year, we sponsor a scholarship for a deserving young woman at the college I attended.

My partner and I are both fourth-generation Vermonters. We are very active in the Historical Association in our town, and since we're the last of the line, except for a few distant cousins, we plan on leaving our home – built by my great-great-grandfather – to be used as a teaching museum when we're gone.

Also, refer back to the question, "What activities do you enjoy?" Is there a way you can share your love of these with a specific population who also would enjoy or benefit from one or more of these activities?

Ok, I admit it. I'm a self-professed math geek. I volunteer at the local high school, which has a large population of "at-risk" kids, and I get them engaged in the Math Club, where we do games, puzzles, and problem solving. I've seen a lot of these kids really come out of their shells. It seems like no one in their life has ever taken the time to engage with them, in learning activities that they also find to be fun. It's my hope that I can encourage at least some of them to stay in school through graduation, and maybe even attend college.

My passion is folk dancing, and I am happy to donate to a local nonprofit organization here in Austin which teaches the elderly how to dance. I just love to see the joy on their faces, as they pick up the steps, and feel a part of our community!

Finding and Working with One or More Organizations

If you don't know where to start to find an organization that's doing the kind of work you'd like to support, or to find an organization near where you live, try searching at GuideStar

USA, Inc. Its mission is: "To revolutionize philanthropy by providing information that advances transparency, enables users to make better decisions, and encourages charitable giving."[6] It offers both free and (advanced) paid versions of its database of most U.S. nonprofit organizations, searchable both by ZIP code, and by interests – so you can begin to see which might be a good match for your time, talents, and treasures.

When Tax Savings Are Not an Issue: Giving to Individuals

Sometimes, the most direct and most rewarding gifts can be those made directly to individuals in need. They may be your neighbors, a young person in your community, or a friend who has experienced a health crisis, job loss, or other personal misfortune.

When I hear of a family down on their luck, I often mail them one or more gift cards to a local supermarket or store, with a note "from a friend." That way, they will not be embarrassed to take a handout, and they can purchase exactly what they need.

Our community set up a members-only website to help those undergoing health treatments, or who are in mourning. We take turns providing dinners every night, and do the weekly marketing, so they can focus on healing.

One of the most meaningful gifts I ever made was to invest in a friend's start-up company. I thought she deserved a chance, and no one else was willing to give it to her. While I had great hope for her success, I gave without any thought of return. Wow, was I surprised years later to find a thank-you letter in the mail – with a check for my original investment plus a 20% return! I immediately took all that money – the principal I

---

[6] www.guidestar.org.

didn't really plan on ever seeing again, plus the generous interest – and donated it to an organization providing seed money for young entrepreneurs.

25 More Ideas for Giving

As you think about choosing recipients for your gifts, perhaps one of these 25 additional giving ideas, arranged from more to less costly and garnered directly from clients and workshop participants (some – in italics – in their own words), will spark your own creative giving practice:

1. Help someone start a micro-business (by purchasing specialized software, a sewing machine and supplies, or cooking equipment, for example).

2. Make a capacity-building grant to a new nonprofit to help them fundraise or hire a marketing consultant; or help a charity by replacing a computer, printer, and/or software.

3. Endow a small scholarship or award at your school to honor a respected teacher or coach.

4. Give your old car, or buy a used one, for a woman getting off public assistance so she can get to her new job.

5. Purchase furniture, kitchen equipment, appliances, or supplies for a halfway house or shelter.

6. *We donated Great-Grandpa's WWI army uniform to the local historical museum. They were very happy to accept it.*

7. Send a child to sleepaway or day YMCA camp for two weeks.

8. Carpet one room at your house of worship.

9. *My sisters and I grew up on the water. When our parents passed away and left us a small sum, we immediately decided to share it in a way that both would honor them and please us and others. So we put our heads together, and decided to buy two canoes for our town's recreation department. Now we can watch youngsters (and some older folks too) learn to enjoy the beautiful lake in a whole new way.*

10. Pay for travel expenses so a nonprofit Executive Director of an organization you support can attend a conference in his/her field.

11. *You know, for just $100, you really can help someone change the direction of his or her life. I managed to save that much this summer by getting off the train one stop early most days and walking the rest of the way. I wanted that hard-earned gift to make a direct impact on someone's life. I also wanted to express my thanks that I have two good legs and I am able to walk. After some research, I found that the career counseling service sponsored by the Combined Jewish Philanthropies will provide an individual with a disability with two hours of career counseling for the price of my gift.*

12. Buy a gift certificate to the Symphony and donate it to a charity auction.

13. Or buy a block of tickets to a sporting event, and donate it to the local Boys and Girls Club.

14. Pay for an instrument rental for one year for an elementary student.

15. Through your local food pantry, donate enough to buy groceries for a small family for one month, one week, or one day.

16. *Everyone in our family loves to picnic near the pond at the old town beach, but it was a hazard for young kids because of all the trash and broken glass. So we started a campaign using email and Facebook, and also sent out notices to the local paper announcing a "Pond Clean Up Day." We bought lots of trash bags and disposable gloves, and refreshments for the volunteers. It cost us less than $75, all told. The town was so grateful, they sent a truck to pick up all the full trash bags!*

17. *During Freshman Orientation Week, our sorority designed and printed three hundred posters and distributed them in area bars near our campus, warning about the dangers of date rape drugs.*

18. *We all love the dance so much! Our young cousin, who has a developmental disability, wanted to come too. When we saw how thrilled and excited she was during the performance, we recognized an opportunity for two nonprofits to team up. We created a program called: "Bring a Buddy to the Ballet." It encourages patrons to buy one extra pair of tickets and donate them to the local social-service agency, to be used by one of their clients with a parent or chaperone. Last season, which was our seventh year, every single child in the program who wanted to go got to see a performance!*

19. *For just $25 or so, you could put together a welcoming basket of toiletries and personal care items for a family moving into a shelter. Or you could create a kids' fun pack with crayons and other art supplies, animal toothbrushes, or an assortment of games and small toys. The shelter director*

let us know that it means the world to displaced children to have something – however tiny – of their very own.

20. Pay to spay or neuter one animal at a local ASPCA.

21. Donate your gently-used books, CDs, or DVDs to the senior center in your town for its lending library. What if your senior center has no lending library? Then go ahead and create one.!

22. *I've always supported the Girl Scouts by buying cookies, but don't need the carbs or the calories! So I bought six boxes of Girl Scout cookies, and immediately dropped them off at the local hospice, which hosts a support group for bereaved children. The cookies were a big hit at snack time!*

23. Say "thanks for your bravery and your service" by surprising your local firefighters or police department with a gift certificate to a nearby pizza or coffee shop (be mindful of the gift rules in your state, which limit the dollar amount they can accept).

24. *There are so many things you can do even with five dollars! You could pick up an extra sandwich for a hungry homeless person, or buy a pair of warm socks, and drop them off at the next clothing drive. Or imagine the delight of an older neighbor or someone else who could use a little cheer, when you present them with a small bouquet of flowers – just because!*

25. *When I give clothes to Goodwill or another charity, I usually slip a coin or two into the pocket. I like to think that the recipient will "pay it forward."*

Consider:

How will you select recipients for your own gifts? What population(s) do you want your gifts to help? If your list is very long, what criteria will you use to narrow the list?

Chapter Six:
What Vehicles for Giving Will You Use?

Once you have selected an organization with a mission that matches your giving goals, the next step is to decide on your vehicle for giving. Here are some questions to consider:

- Do you prefer to make a gift of time or expertise, cash, goods, or securities?

- Do you wish to make the gift now, all at once, or over a period of time, or after you are deceased, as a bequest from your estate?

- Do you prefer to know specifically how your donation will be used (designated gift), or is it OK with you to let the organization decide how best to use your gift (unrestricted)?

- Will you give directly to the organization of your choice, or will you join other like-minded individuals in donating to a federated fund or community foundation, via a giving circle, or by a charity crowdfunding appeal?

Give Directly to the Charity of Your Choice

For most of us, the most familiar way to give is to donate directly to the charity of choice. Gifts can be made in cash – such as the dollar you drop into the "support our high school athletic programs" canister at the local market checkout – or by check or credit card or online.

Or you can give household items, such as used clothing, to the Red Cross, or better work clothes to Career Gear, or furniture to Big Brothers or the Veterans Association of America, who will come and pick it up.

In the past several years, crowdfunding — that is, funding a business, project, or artistic venture by raising many small donations from a large number of people, usually via social media — has been used successfully for charitable causes. You will read more about this in Chapter Ten.

You also can make donations of property, including securities or real estate. A different tax structure may apply to these gifts, so it is always a good idea to check with your tax advisor before making such a gift.

I've been a big fan of Peets Coffee since the late 1960s. When the company went public in 2001, I bought as much stock as I could afford. Then, when the company went private in 2012, I was forced to sell my stock. I was left with an expensive "first-world" problem: the large capital gains tax. To avoid paying the tax, I decided transfer some shares to each of a few favorite charities. Unfortunately, some of the smaller charities I support were not set up to receive gifts of securities, so they couldn't benefit.

If you decide to make a gift of cash or securities, there are many different ways your gift can help. By letting the organization know of your preference, either online or via a note or phone call, you can designate that your gift be used in one or more of these ways:

Operations. The ongoing, day-to-day costs of running the organization, including salaries, rent, utilities, insurance, and other recurring expenses. Usually, unless you designate your gift for some other purpose, it will be used to pay for operations, since this tends to be the most challenging area for most organizations to fund.

Programs. Providing direct services to clients, or for research. This can include salaries, supplies, travel, and other funds necessary to carry out a specific project or program.

Seed money. Support to help an organization get started, or to help start an organization's brand-new initiative.

Capacity building. Support to help the organization build its ability to operate more effectively or efficiently. For example, hiring a consultant to advise on or assist with operations, board development, media relations, marketing, graphic design, or fundraising; or upgrading computers, the phone system, or fundraising software.

Technical support. Web design, social media, advertising design and placement.

Capital expenses. Buildings, land, major equipment.

Emergency funds. For any unforeseen events or needs occurring outside the organization's normal operations, which are expected to be a temporary or one-time situation. For example, a recently hired senior staff person resigns suddenly, and the organization has not yet saved up enough reserve funds to conduct a new search.

Sponsorships. Support for a single event, such as engaging a youth group to partner with your neighborhood to do a community playground clean up. You pay for the trash bags and other supplies, while the organization secures and supervises the volunteers.

Endowment funds. Gifts are invested for the organization's future use. Normally, the capital is left untouched, and only the interest is used. Sometimes, a small, specific amount of the capital (3% is typical) is drawn down annually.

A challenge grant, also known as matching funds. You offer to donate a specific amount of money – either for operations, or more often, for a specific project – once the organization can raise the same amount, or a predetermined percentage of that amount, on its own. Example: you offer to match all new member gifts to the Friends of the Library, within a specific time period, up to a specific amount.[7]

---

[7] This section is adapted from *Get That Grant: The Quick-Start Guide to Successful Proposals, Second Edition*, by Gail R. Shapiro and Carla C. Cataldo, (BookLocker, 2009), and used with the kind permission of my co-author.

Give to a Federated Fund, Community Foundation, or Other Public Foundation

A federated giving program is a joint fundraising effort usually administered by a nonprofit or government "umbrella" organization that in turn distributes the contributed funds to several nonprofit agencies. United Way and community chests or funds, the U.S. government's Combined Federal Campaign, the United Jewish Appeal and other religious appeals, the United Negro College Fund, and joint arts councils are examples of federated giving programs. Some federated giving programs have a particular focus. For example, Community Shares USA is a collaboration of organizations "committed to achieving fairness and opportunity for all." Supported through workplace giving, member groups from all over the country "support a variety of community-based organizations and causes" which "play a vital role in advancing social, economic and environmental issues in their own communities." [8]

Community foundations are local charitable entities that may administer a number of endowed funds specifically created to fund local causes. Most large cities and many regions now have community foundations. Donors can make an unrestricted gift to be used wherever the foundation managers think best, or a designated gift, to a particular charity or field of interest. Or you could create a donor-advised fund within the community foundation for any purpose you choose (see below).

You also may choose to support a public foundation, which is a public charity established to address a particular issue, such as arts education, or to support the needs of a specific population, such as women and girls. Many donors contribute funds to the foundation, which then makes the selection of specific charities and gives them grants. Community foundations sometimes favor making capacity-building grants to nonprofits, and also may

---

[8] http://communitysharesusa.org.

sponsor workshops and training to building the capacity of the organizations in their geographic area.

Donor-advised funds are accounts established at a public charity, such as a community foundation, which allows a donor to make a charitable contribution, receive an immediate tax benefit, and then recommend grants from the fund immediately or at a future date. The foundation administers your fund, usually for a small yearly fee. According to the National Philanthropic Trust, "an easy way to think about a donor-advised fund is like a charitable savings account: a donor contributes to the fund as frequently as they like and then recommends grants to their favorite charity when they are ready."[9]

In the past twenty years or so, these funds have grown rapidly in popularity, and now account for more than three percent of all charitable giving in the U.S.

Women's funds. During the past 40 years, in response to the need to address the special funding requirements of programs serving women and girls, the giving vehicle known as the women's fund was created. A women's fund combines individual gifts, gifts from smaller family foundations, as well as corporate gifts, and then disburses grants to nonprofit organizations whose programs help meet the specific needs of this population.

Women's funds can be structured in one of several ways: as community foundations, as private foundations, as a federation of member groups, or as designated funds within community or public foundations. Although the funds may differ in structure, and in geographic and programmatic focus, they have much in common with one another.

---

[9] National Philanthropic Trust (www.nptrust.org).

Generally, they involve women in decision making, both in the distribution of funds, and in the focus of the organization. They work to increase the number of donors, they seek to expand opportunities for women and girls, and they tend to support women's empowerment and participation, as well as addressing discrimination. In addition to making grants for programs that support women and girls, women's funds may sponsor workshops on a wide variety of topics; operate a "skills bank" available to community women; offer technical assistance; spearhead coalitions among community groups around a common cause; honor women leaders; publish magazines, blogs, newsletters, and books; offer webinars and sponsor conferences; and promote philanthropy among women. Each foundation has its own focus. Larger foundations make many grants throughout the year to several organizations, while smaller foundations may have a more narrow focus and scope.

In 1985, some of the existing women's funds joined together to form the National Network of Women's Funds, now called the Women's Funding Network (www.womensfundingnetwork.org). From five member organizations in 1979, to 40 in 1987, to more than 100 women's funds and foundations in 40 countries today, the WFN is the largest philanthropic network in the world devoted to women and girls.[10]

Set Up Your Own Foundation

While beyond the financial scope of "small gifts" that is the focus of this book, setting up a foundation – that is, creating a separate legal vehicle for your giving – is mentioned here briefly, because some may be intrigued with the associated prestige and benefits. These include: providing for the long-term needs of organizations and people you want to help, creating a legacy to

---

[10] This section is adapted from *Money Order: The Money Management Guide for Women*. Womankind Educational and Resource Center, Inc. Gail R. Shapiro, editor. Simon & Schuster, 2001.

honor a family member, and tax advantages. Since the legal and tax ramifications are so complicated, most philanthropic advisors suggest that this vehicle be considered only by those with several hundred thousands of dollars in assets, or by those who intend to donate more than $50,000 dollars a year.

Planned Giving

Named because it generally requires more thought, planning, and execution than simply writing a check to a charitable organization, a planned gift usually is defined as a gift that you create during your lifetime, with final disposition when you die. While a description of the various vehicles also is beyond this book's scope, planned gifts may include, among others: a simple bequest in a will or trust or within an estate plan, charitable gift annuities, charitable remainder trusts, charitable lead trusts, non-cash assets, and assets transferred using pay-on-death or transfer-on-death documents.

Planned giving can make it possible for you to give to the charity of your choice, meet your own current or future income needs, and also provide for your heirs. You may designate one or more nonprofit organizations, your own private foundation, your local community foundation or other public foundation, or your own supporting organization to receive the benefits of your planned gifts. Consult your financial advisor or estate planning attorney for more information on these vehicles.

Create Your Own Project by Identifying Needs

Perhaps you now have some idea of which population or populations, or which organization(s) you'd like to support. You then can decide how you'd like to support that organization or population: writing a check, making an online gift, or donating your time, household goods, or equipment. But what if you have not yet found a good match for your gifts? There are several other ways you can donate.

From the very simplest project, to creating your own nonprofit organization and perhaps employing hundreds of individuals, non-cash gifts most often require some planning and community involvement. You can start a drive to collect coats for the homeless, or musical instruments for underfunded schools, or you can organize a quilting bee to create a quilt to be auctioned for charity. You could "adopt" a classroom in a low-income community, and purchase supplies, or start an after-school reading program. The possibilities are endless. Below are a few examples which may inspire you.

Respond to a Disaster on Your Own

In the wake of the 2005 Hurricane Katrina disaster, Nadine Nesbitt of Ashland, MA didn't wait for "the authorities" to help. "Why do we have to give to the Red Cross and wait for them to help out?" said Ms. Nesbitt, founder of WAITT ("We're All in This Together"), a unique marketing company, and founder and former owner of Purple Ink Insurance Agency, Inc.

She called Baton Rouge shelters until she found one couple eager to move north to start over. She sent plane tickets, and offered an apartment in her newly purchased three-family house. The residents of Ashland, where Ms. Nesbitt is active in the local Business Association, all pitched in with electrical work, furnishings, clothing, and job offers. This couple knew of other hurricane-displaced families in need, and eventually, four families were relocated to the Ashland area.

Ms. Nesbitt, the mother of four, is self-effacing about her generosity. "It isn't amazing – it's what we as Americans are supposed to do," she said in a newspaper interview. "These people are living in shelters with no shoes. These people lost their lives right here in our country. There's no magic potion or secret to help fix the problem. That's what 'We the People' is all about." [11]

Start Your Own Nonprofit Organization

When Zachary Hicks was in seventh grade, he began to notice the contrasts between the "haves" and the "have-nots." Less than ten miles from his affluent home town were schools where the students had few books, and the school libraries had no budget. As a Bar Mitzvah project, he started the Share-A-Book Foundation, a nonprofit organization which "promotes literacy and the joy of reading among young children in disadvantaged communities" in Essex County, New Jersey, where Mr. Hicks grew up, and where the literacy rate is less than half the national average. Through book drives at area schools and houses of worship, and in partnership with other area nonprofits, his foundation collected and distributed more than 30,000 new and gently used books to children.

Eventually partnering with United Way, Mr. Hicks also encouraged young volunteers to read to children in recipient schools, an experience which he said, "has enabled me and the other volunteers to grow in innumerable ways. I have learned to interact with and appreciate people of different races and cultures, as we share our mutual love of reading."

His hope was that the impact of the foundation would be long term, as these same children will "grow with the ability to read and will share that ability with others in their community." In 2004, at the age of 16, Zachary Hicks was named a Daily Point of Light for his volunteer service by President George W. Bush.

---

[11] Megan Tench, "Mass. residents open their hearts, homes," *The Boston Globe.* Sept. 7, 2005.

His lifelong enthusiasm for volunteering continued throughout his years at Colgate University, where he was a founding member of Colgate's bike share program called Green Bikes. Today, as an assistant vice president in the insurance industry, Mr. Hicks has made time to sit on various charity committees for his employers, to participate in helping refugees (particularly from Burma) become acquainted with life in the United States, and to help maintain outdoor trail networks by working with the National Forest Service. As a relatively new resident of his community, he says he is challenging himself "to integrate with people of all backgrounds throughout the community, so I can leave an impact in my new town, as well as making the city feel more like home."

For more information on how to start your own nonprofit organization, see Chapter Ten.

Offer the Gift of Kindness

Even when funds are tight, your schedule doesn't offer time for volunteer work, and you are making do with (instead of donating) your old boots, there still are many ways to express your charitable intent.

Children learn (or don't learn) kindness and tolerance not only from tangible giving but also from the way we treat other people: our kindness in just saying hello to a homeless person and meeting her or his gaze, instead of looking away. Or letting someone who looks frazzled cut in front of us in line. Or being patient with a new cashier learning the job.

Responsive Giving

Whichever vehicle you decide to use for giving, you also may want to consider reserving a small percentage of your charitable budget for spontaneous, responsive giving. Your neighbor's child may approach you to support her in a school fundraiser, or your spouse's employer may ask everyone at the office to donate to her charity marathon run. Even though these causes may not match your own giving goals, you occasionally may want to make a small gift to respond to requests of those who are important to you.

Consider:

What vehicles will you use for giving? How might you use the ideas in this chapter to spark more creative giving? How can you take the information you've learned about yourself and your giving priorities in these first six chapters and turn it into your Personal Charitable Giving Plan?

Part Two:
Your Giving in Action

Giving money effectively is almost as hard as earning it in the first place.

- **Bill Gates**

Chapter Seven:
Evaluating Charitable Organizations

Not too long ago, I was browsing in a small new bookshop in a nearby town. The proprietor, "Jerry," a young man of about 25, was helping another customer at the desk, when in swept a very tall, imposing figure in a clerical collar.

Without waiting for an invitation, the minister ("just call me Rev Bill") proceeded to deliver an impassioned request for funds to support his church in the poorest section of the city, never seeming to stop for breath as he described the various programs of his church and how they were helping the needy. He then went on to explain to Jerry that ***every other*** business on the block already had given, and moreover, had been giving regularly for many years. He finished with a pitch for funds that, at least to me, sounded more like intimidation than a request.

The young business owner, who clearly looked uneasy and even a bit frightened, opened up the register, and handed the visitor a couple of twenty-dollar bills. Blessing and thanking him, the fellow left.

When the other customer left, I approached Jerry.

"Did you know that man?"

"No."

"Do you know whether your neighbors actually support his church?"

"No."

"Did he show you any identification? Any brochure or material from his 'church?'"

"Um, no," he admitted sheepishly, the truth beginning to dawn on him.

"Looks like you were embarrassed not to give in front of your regular customer."

"Well, yeah. And he was a little scary."

"Did you get a receipt at least?"

No again.

Unfortunately, Jerry's experience is not uncommon. While the solicitor may indeed have been a legitimate minister from a recognized church who would actually use the funds for good, Jerry didn't have any way to know that. And the simple fact that materials were not proffered, nor a receipt given or promised, looks like Jerry may have been scammed.

While not all requests you receive are so dramatic, you do need to exercise care before you give. How can you tell if a request for funds is legitimate? And whether the organization receiving the funds is a real charity, which will use your gift well and appropriately?

When you are approached in person, on the phone, by email, or by letter, your first step should be to determine whether the organization soliciting you is indeed registered with the IRS as a 501(c)(3) charitable organization. To do so, you have three options:

- **Contact** the organization yourself and ask to see its IRS letter recognizing it as tax-exempt.
- **Confirm** the organization's status by calling the IRS at 1-877-829-5500 during normal business hours, or by visiting the IRS website (www.IRS.gov).
- **Visit** the GuideStar website (www.guidestar.org), which lists more than 1.8 million IRS-registered organizations, plus thousands of religious organizations, which are tax-exempt by definition, and not required to apply to the IRS for exemption.

In all three cases, not all charitable organizations are listed, either because they are too small, or because, although they have a not-for-profit mission, they may not be incorporated as an officially recognized nonprofit.

To obtain nonprofit status from the IRS, in all but ten states, a new organization first must incorporate following the laws in its home state. It then may apply to the IRS for nonprofit status, which, if granted, will confer tax benefits both to the organization and also, normally, to its donors (depending on the donors' own tax situation).

The process is lengthy, and requires that the organization file its Articles of Incorporation, bylaws, and very detailed information about its finances, its programs, and purpose. If approved – a process which can take six to nine months, sometimes longer – the organization will receive provisional status. After the provisional period ends, if the IRS is satisfied that the organization is following state law, and is meeting its test as a nonprofit (the percentage of donations received from the public, among others), it will be granted permanent status under IRS regulation 501(c)(3).

Next, visit the organization's website. What can you learn about it and how it works? You'll want to look for:

- A clear, compelling **mission statement**.

- **Clientele**. Who the organization serves, as well as its service area.

- **Administration**. Who oversees the operations of the organization? You should be able to see the names of the Executive Director, senior staff, and members of the Board of Directors.

- **Financial information**. At a minimum, look at the organization's most recent IRS 990 filings (the form filed by a nonprofit even though it is not required to pay taxes). This document should be available on the organization's website, but if not, it can be obtained from the organization upon request. Larger and long-established organizations also should post their audited financial statements. Note executive pay, amounts spent on fundraising, administration, and programs, and the types of support the organization receives (government, program income, corporate, foundation, and public donations).

- **Policies** in place to protect clients and donors, such as donor privacy policies (will your name be sold or swapped with another nonprofit?), as well as a conflict of interest policy for Board and staff.

How can you evaluate this information? There are no "one-size-fits-all" right answers, so you must use your own judgment. Clearly, it is less compelling to find that your gift may be used for overhead expenses, instead of, say, feeding hungry children. Yet without rent, lights, and salaries, the organization cannot do its work.

While there are several websites that seek to help donors by rating charities, it's preferable to do your own research if you can. Some of these sites use financial information self-reported by the charity, and do not verify it. Others may not take into account the value of volunteer time when looking at a charity's finances, or they may place too much weight on the "administration-to-services" spending ratio, when those are just part of the picture. An Executive Director tells this story:

One prospective donor to our new organization said he looked us up [on a charity rating website] and refused to give because he "was horrified" to find that 85% of our funds went for administration. He then proceeded to scream at me for five full minutes, accusing me of ripping off the kids we were serving, and the whole community, with my "ridiculously high salary." I let him finish his rant, then patiently explained that as the founder and part-time Executive Director, I took no salary at all; that we were just starting our second full year of operations, and the numbers he was seeing on the charity evaluation website were from our first year, when we spent nearly all our funds renting space and buying a few used computers, so we could start tutoring kids immediately, and the rest was spent on website design. He was very quiet, then apologized profusely and said he would send a check right away.

How can you tell if an organization is meeting its mission, that is, if its programs and services are effective and meeting both its own benchmarks and the needs of the community? How can you find this information if it is not readily available? Here are a few tips:

- **Call the organization.**

Ask to speak to the Executive Director, or to the financial officer. Ask them to share with you the organization's Strategic

Plan, or any internal documents that will give you the information you seek. Even if these documents are not readily available (for example, the organization may be in the process of updating its Strategic Plan), you can tell a lot from how your request is handled and answered.

- **Look for its public donors**.

While the organization does not disclose the names of individual donors like you, to protect privacy, it usually does make public the names of corporations and foundations from which it receives grants. Look for a list of the organization's larger corporate and foundation funders. These normally can be found either on the charity's own website or in its Annual Report (they also are listed on Guidestar.org). Sometimes, just seeing which corporations and foundations have made large gifts to the organization under your consideration can help you feel reassured that your funds will be used well, as it is not unreasonable to assume that these larger donors have done proper due diligence.

- **Make a personal site visit**.

If feasible, make an appointment and go visit the organization's office or physical program site. Look around. Ask questions. If appropriate, ask to speak directly to the clients it serves. Talk with the staff. Use your own common sense and good judgment to determine if you like what you see.

The key principle in evaluating charities is **complete transparency**. Everything you want or need to know to feel secure about making a donation should be readily available to you: either on the organization's website, or provided at your request.

Once you are comfortable – or as sure as you can be – that your gift will be used well, do go ahead and give freely.

Reviewing Your Choices

Once you've created and are using your Charitable Giving Plan, you can always change your mind, and make a different choice next time around. In fact, it's a good idea to review your choices, at least every few years, if not more often. When might you decide to change the recipients for your gifts?

- **When Your Giving Priorities Change**.

What once was important to you may no longer be so. You may have supported your son's Little League Team, and now he's playing soccer, or he's grown and gone off to college. You may have changed religious congregations, and so want to direct your gifts to your new spiritual home. You may have lost a family member to illness, and want to give some of your charitable dollars to finding a cure for that disease. Your political views may have shifted, or the hobby you found so compelling for many years no longer interests you.

- **The Leadership or Mission of the Organization May Change**.

You may no longer agree with the new direction of the organization, and want to vote with your dollars against the new policy.

My alma mater banned fraternities from campus this year. Greek life was a very important part of my college experience – I made lifelong friends, as well as plentiful business opportunities, and an excellent network of contacts. I did register my views with the administration, but did not get what I considered to be a satisfactory response. So not only did I stop making an annual gift after almost 50 years, I also changed my bequest, so that now the college will not get any money from me after I die.

• **You Feel Disrespected**.

The organization may be sending you far too many solicitations, and will not stop even when you've asked them to do so. Or they may have sold or traded your name, and you are now getting solicitations from similar organizations – so many that you feel overwhelmed by them all.

I just don't know what to do now. I made a gift to a local animal shelter, and now I'm getting mailings and requests from so many animal and environmental charities I don't know or care about. I really hate what [first organization] did – releasing my contact information without my permission.

If you have been added to a charity's mail list without your specific permission, and without having made a donation, clip the printed address from the last mailing, and mail it back to the charity with a note requesting that you be removed from their list immediately. Sometimes you may have to do this more than once.

If you suspect or you know where that charity got your name, you also should contact the original charity (the one you likely are supporting) and request that your name no longer be sold or traded.

You also can add your home and cell phone numbers to the Federal Trade Commission's National "Do Not Call" Registry (www.donotcall.gov), which is designed to prevent all unwanted solicitation calls.

• **You Learn That Your Donation Has Been Misused – or Worse.**

I opened the morning paper not too long ago, to find that the bookkeeper for a veterans group I'd been supporting had been arrested for embezzling more than three quarters of a million dollars from the organization during the past several years. Apparently, she wrote more than 100 checks to herself and her family for cash, and used the organization's credit cards to pay for travel, purchases, and other personal expenses. Wasn't anybody paying attention?

Should you learn or believe that a charity's activities are not on the up-and-up, what can you do? Your first call should be to the Attorney General's office in your state, which regulates charitable organizations. The specific office to contact may have a different name in each state, such as: Public Charities Division (Massachusetts), Registry of Charitable Trusts (California), or Charitable Trust Section (Michigan), and a simple online search will help you find the right listing. Most of these offices have on their websites the steps you should follow to report known or suspected fraud.

But what of an organization which is legitimate, but is one you don't wish to support, either right now, in the near future, or ever? Just as important as deciding how to say "yes" to an organization that meets your giving priorities, is how to say "no."

Many people have a tough time saying "no." Paid charity telephone solicitors are trained to answer nearly every single objection raised by those they call, but I've found that there is one refusal they just can't answer.

It's the same one I use almost daily during the busy fall giving season, from kids going door-to-door selling wrapping paper, to the cashier at the supermarket asking if I'd like to donate a dollar to support the company's foundation, to the guy ringing the bell for the Salvation Army – all presumably good and worthy causes. My "no" is this:

"It's not in my Charitable Giving Plan."

Depending on who's asking (child, cashier I see regularly, neighbor) and for what (cause to which I have no objection, but about which I don't particularly care), that line sometimes is preceded with a "Sorry," or delivered with a rueful smile, if I do indeed think their charity or cause is worthwhile and I'm just so sorry I'm not going to help.

Sometimes, the line is followed with "this year" ("It's not in my Charitable Giving Plan *this year*") if indeed it is a charity I might possibly consider in the future.

If the asker persists, just repeat the line – more than once, if necessary – and know that you've made the very best decision as to how to spend your charitable dollars. That same line also works well if you are asked to chair a committee, bake brownies for the school fair, or help sort books for the library book sale.

Again, should the asker continue, remember that "No." is a complete sentence. Being confident that you've made the right choices for you will give you the confidence to say "no" to the causes that are not the best match for you right now.

Consider:

How will you evaluate the nonprofit organizations or causes you are considering? Are you confident that your gifts will be spent wisely? If not, what else could you do to find out more? Are you comfortable saying "no" to people, charities, or causes you do not wish to support? If not, what can you do to become more confident?

__When you cease to make a contribution, you begin to die.__

- **Eleanor Roosevelt**

Chapter Eight:
Volunteering: Your Energy Is a Resource Too!

When I turned 50, I estimated the number of hours I'd spent as a volunteer: from selling Girl Scout cookies and collecting for UNICEF each Halloween – right on up to founding a new nonprofit. I then looked up the value of a volunteer hour (for each year, going way back) and was stunned to learn that I'd given away more than a million dollars' worth of my time! I felt very good about myself, plus, I found it very easy to say "no" the next time I was asked to chair a committee.

Who volunteers?

In 2015, nearly 63 million Americans volunteered 7.9 billion hours, according to the Corporation for National and Community Service. Based on an estimate of $23.56 as the current average value of a volunteer hour, Americans donated almost $184 billion that year.[12]

We are all familiar – and fairly comfortable with – the role of women as volunteers. Brownie leaders, den mothers, hospital "pink ladies" or "Candystripers," Junior League thrift shop managers, library pages, voter registration workers, ESL tutors, phonathon callers, school trip chaperones, and bakers of endless cupcakes: these are only some of the ways American women have given of themselves throughout the years.

---

[12] Corporation for National and Community Service, "Volunteering and Civic Life in America 2015" (www.volunteeringinamerica.gov), April 2016.

The stereotypical image of men as volunteers has been that of the retiree, driving the local Council On Aging van, working as a docent at the art museum, or chairing a congregational fundraising committee. But that's no longer the case.

While it is true that for a long time, men volunteered at a much lower rate than women, in recent years, the gap has narrowed somewhat.

According to a 2016 report by the U.S. Department of Labor,[13] of the 62.6 million people who volunteered through or for an organization at least once in the year ending September 2015, the rate for men was 21.8%, and 27.8% for women. Across all age groups, educational levels, and other major demographic characteristics, women continued to volunteer at a higher rate than men.

The study also shows that volunteer activities differed among men and women. Men were most likely to engage in general labor (12.3%); or coach, referee, or supervise sports teams (9.3%); or collect, prepare, distribute, or serve food (9.2%). Women were most likely to collect, prepare, distribute, or serve food (12.9%); tutor or teach (10.6%); or fundraise (9.9%).[14]

In addition to gender differences, there also are significant age differences in volunteers. It is not a surprise that the largest median number of volunteer hours (100 per year) is donated by those aged 75 and older – presumably, since they are retired and have more time to give. But what may be a surprise is that Generation X (born approximately 1963 to 1979), had the highest volunteer rate of all age groups at 30%, while one in five

---

[13] U.S. Department of Labor, Bureau of Labor Statistics, "Volunteering in the United States, 2015". February 25, 2016.

[14] Ibid.

Millennials (born approximately 1980 to 1995) volunteered in 2014.[15]

The top four national volunteer activities are: fundraising or selling items to raise money (25.7%), food collection or distribution (23.8%), general labor or transportation (19.8%), and tutoring or teaching (17.9%). The top four volunteer areas are for: religious (34.2%), educational (26.5%), social service (14.4%), and health (8.0%) organizations.[16]

So no matter what your age, or where your interests lie, there is sure to be a volunteer opportunity that is right for you.

Why Volunteer?

In addition to the many benefits volunteering provides to the organizations served, their clients, and their communities, volunteering also offers many benefits to you, the volunteer. Among them are:

Improve Your Mental and Physical Health

Many researchers find that volunteering – both in an organized way, and expressed in small good deeds – is good for the giver's mental and physical well-being:

Sonja Lyubomirsky, Ph.D., Professor at UC Riverside: "[...] you don't have to be a Mother Teresa or the Dalai Lama; the acts can be small and brief" (p. 133). And, "timing is everything." In one experiment, she reports, those who designated a certain day

---

[15] Corporation for National and Community Service, op. cit.

[16] Ibid.

a week for acts of kindness were happier than those who spread them out over the whole week. [17]

Monica Bartlett and David DeSteno, Department of Psychology, Northeastern University: "Volunteering is associated with diminished depression, and enhanced feelings of self-worth, mastery, and personal control. This has been called a 'helper's high.'"[18]

Christopher Peterson: "Volunteer work is associated with high life satisfaction and good health..." (p. 257). "One of the solid findings of positive psychology is that an orientation to the welfare of others is in the long run more satisfying than an orientation to one's own pleasure. Philanthropy brings more happiness than self-oriented fun" (p. 34).[19]

Sociologists Christian Smith and Hilary Davidson, at Notre Dame's Science of Generosity Initiative, found that "generous people, on the whole, were happier and healthier and had a greater sense of purpose than others, even after controlling for a number of factors, including income." And "those who describe themselves as 'very happy' volunteer an average of 5.8 hours per month, while those who self-describe as 'unhappy' give 0.6 hours."[20]

---

[17] Sonja Lyubomirsky. *The How of Happiness*, Penguin Press HC. December, 2007, p 125-135.

[18] Monica Bartlett and David DeSteno. "Gratitude and prosocial behavior: Helping when it costs you." Psychological Science, 17:4. Association for Psychological Science, 2006 (p. 130-132).

[19] Christopher Peterson. *A Primer in Positive Psychology*. Oxford Positive Psychology Series. Oxford University Press. July 27, 2006.

[20] Christian Smith and Hilary Davidson. *The Paradox of Generosity: Giving We Receive, Grasping We Lose*. Oxford University Press, September, 2014.

Gain Valuable Skills and Work Experience

At least one study shows that volunteers have a 27% higher chance of finding a paying job after being out of work.[21] Volunteering in a position with transferable skills can help you become more experienced when you are looking for that job. This is especially true if you have just finished school, or if you've been out of the work force for some time, for example, to raise children.

Volunteer experience can be invaluable: to expand your personal network, put yourself into a new environment, watch how others work, and interact with those in parallel positions, as well as provide the opportunity to supervise others, thus developing your leadership skills.

If you find that your volunteer work does not challenge you, don't be shy about asking for a more demanding assignment. Should the hours you are being asked to work not fit with your own work or family schedule, you may be able to negotiate a better schedule. You can view every step of the volunteer experience as practice for your own next job: from meeting your commitment to negotiating for more responsibility to learning how to network.

Plus, volunteering offers you the opportunity to experiment with a new field or new endeavor, or try something in which you're interested. This way, if you don't like it, you'll know before you take classes or apply for the job, and then realize it's not what you want to do as a career.

---

[21] Christopher Spera, Ph.D.; Robin Ghertner, M.P.P.; Anthony Nerino, M.A.; Adrienne DiTommaso, M.P.A. "Volunteering as a Pathway to Employment: Does Volunteering Increase Odds of Finding a Job for the Out of Work?" Corporation for National and Community Service, Office of Research and Evaluation, Washington, D.C., June 2013.

Enhance Your Resume

Again, both for new graduates and for stay-at-home parents returning to the workforce, volunteer work looks good on your resume. If you are still in high school, and thinking of applying to college, know that most colleges and universities ask for or even require community service. Since college admissions are increasingly competitive, it's not a bad idea to think about a way to make your volunteer work fill an important community need or address a problem.

"Ten-day spring break trips to foreign countries to dig ditches, with essays about how this experience was life-changing, seem to show up on lots of applications from the top suburban high schools in wealthier communities," says one highly selective college's admissions director, who asked to remain anonymous. *"We'd rather see a long commitment to filling an actual need in the applicant's own community – or even within his or her own family, such as helping to care for a disabled sibling or an elderly grandparent, or holding down a part-time job to help out if a parent has lost his or her job."*

Make New Friends and Potential Mentors

Not only do you gain experience, but you may meet people who can be potential references when you are job hunting, assuming you made the right impression. Or they may help by recommending someplace to apply for a job. Let them know you are looking, and ask if they will be on your list of references, after you've shown them what you can do.

Even when you are not looking for a job, or seeking to enhance your resume, volunteering has many other benefits.

Get to Know More about Your Community

Whether you've just moved to a new city or town, or want to get more involved in the place you've lived for years, volunteering is a great way to deepen your relationship to your home, and work for causes that benefit you and your neighbors.

Change Your Career and Your Life

"In 1988, I didn't know that I was starting anything," says Reverend Maddie Sifantus, founder of the Wayland, Massachusetts-based Golden Tones Chorus, a group of nearly 70 retired men and women who love to sing and dance, and who perform 50 concerts each year in residences for senior citizens, and also in schools, faith communities, and public settings.

Now minister of the Unitarian Universalist Church in Santa Paula, California, Reverend Sifantus, a professional singer by training, says, "I did it to give back – to bring joy [to others] through my voice."

The daughter of two musicians who joined her in her initial efforts to engage elders in bringing music to their cohorts, Reverend Sifantus at that time was a divorced mother in her 30s, and had not completed a college degree. She recognized a community need: for elders like her parents, as well as amateur and aspiring music-makers, to engage socially by making and performing music, while having fun, lifting their own and their audiences' spirits, and creating a community.

"I just gathered a small group which met at our local Council On Aging," she explained, "and we sang the songs they loved from their youth, and songs they remembered their own parents singing. Within six months of our first meeting, we grew from a group of ten to twenty, then to fifty within two years."

"We decided to incorporate as a nonprofit when people started wanting to support us with donations," she says. "Every time we rehearsed, or held a sing-a-long, folks would ask how they could help. And we kept getting requests from nursing homes and senior living centers for performances."

At the same time, Reverend Sifantus was inspired to return to college, and earned first a BS, then an MA, from Lesley University, with a specialization in Elder Studies. Through her work with the Golden Tones, she felt a calling to the ministry. She then completed her Masters in Divinity from Andover Newton Theological School, and was ordained as a Unitarian Universalist minister in affiliation with the First Parish in Wayland, where the Golden Tones Chorus is still going strong under the aegis of a new director.

How to Volunteer

As you think about possible volunteer opportunities, consider:
- How involved would you like to be?
- How much time would you prefer to give?
- Will you give a regular time weekly or monthly, or donate a day, a weekend, or a week as needed? Do you want to do direct hands-on work with the clients, technical work, or offer office help, such as doing periodic mailings?
- Would you prefer to donate your professional expertise (legal, financial management, administrative, marketing, or fundraising) or serve on a Board of Directors?

Before You Volunteer

To get the most out of your experience, ask yourself the questions on this worksheet before you get involved with an organization:

**WORKSHEET FOUR:
THINKING ABOUT VOLUNTEERING**

What have I done in the past that I've enjoyed?

What do I want to do as a volunteer, and what would I rule out doing?

How much time can I commit? What are my schedule constraints?

What talents or skills can I offer?

What kinds of people do I want to work with?

What would I most like to learn by volunteering?

Finding and Evaluating Volunteer Opportunities in Your Community

If you are naturally an outgoing person, you might start by asking your friends, neighbors, colleagues, even everyone you meet: "I'm looking for an interesting new volunteer opportunity. Do you volunteer? Will you tell me about it?"

I've always supported Special Olympics, and volunteered several hours a week. But when my daughter became a toddler, it became impossible to bring her. So they found a way for me to volunteer online, and I can do the work while she naps or in the evenings.

I was so amazed to find out that my elderly next-door neighbor, who I always thought of as needing help, actually was spending two days a week at the local hospital, holding and rocking the preterm babies. In addition, using her experience as a retired biology professor, she mentors two young women at the high school, who also aspire to be scientists.

You also could begin your search online. There are many databases which sort volunteer opportunities by geographic locale, area of interest, and who needs help. In addition, you can use the GuideStar database[22] to find organizations in your community which may be in need of volunteers.

Volunteering as a Family

In addition to the many benefits of volunteering already described, volunteering as a family offers additional rewards:

- Children and adults feel valued and important, and can gain new skills and experiences.

---

[22] www.guidestar.org.

- Parents can share their values and engage in meaningful conversations, while spending high-quality time with their children.

- Everyone develops understanding and compassion for others – good lifelong qualities to have.

- Nonprofits get "hands-on" help, as well as the ability to integrate volunteers of all ages into their organization.

- The larger community reaps the reward of another generation of micro-philanthropists, as extensive research shows that children who volunteer are very likely to continue to do so as adults.

My teenaged son, who has high-functioning autism, really wanted to be able to help the less fortunate, but we couldn't find any organization that was willing to take the "risk" they felt he might pose. Boy, was that a disappointment! Fortunately, right about this time, our church sponsored a mission trip to work in an orphanage in the Dominican Republic during summer vacation. My son and I worked together in the large kitchen preparing three meals each day. We fell into bed exhausted each night – it was hard work! – but with the satisfaction you get from a job well done. Looking back now, I honestly think this was the very best thing for his own development, self-confidence, and self-esteem. After a lifetime of being bullied and teased, he was treated with respect and dignity by the orphanage director, and the gratitude from the staff, and even the children, just put the biggest grin on his face!

When my kids were small, we often drove to the children's room in the library of a nearby town. We would take a few new dollar bills, maybe five or so, and slip one into each of our favorite books. We'd then have a great time on the way home and for days afterward, thinking about the delight of the children who found the money, and how maybe they would tell their friends, and then all the kids would rush to the library, and get more interested in reading!

You can find family volunteer opportunities using the same internet search, using the search term "volunteer opportunities for families." While it may take a few tries, with some effort, you can find a good volunteer match for you and your family. The rewards are worth it!

Consider:

Does adding volunteering to your Charitable Giving Plan make sense for you? If so, where might you begin to look for a good opportunity? What is your main purpose for wanting to volunteer? What interests you, and how can you best be of service to your community?

It's easy to make a buck. It's a lot tougher to make a difference.

- Tom Brokaw

Chapter Nine:
Giving When You Own a Small Business

Owners of both large and small businesses often are approached for contributions to Little League teams, "Las Vegas Nights" for a local parish, or a silent auction for the Garden Club; or to buy chocolate bars, plastic wrist bands, or even bottled water to send the cheerleading squad to the state competition or the school band on its annual trip to Washington, D.C.

Many business owners give to everyone who walks in the door, wanting to be thought of as a good neighbor in the community that supports them and their business. That's not always the best policy, as one retail business owner explains:

The vast majority of those soliciting donations are looking for gift certificates or merchandise, not cash. Most are schools; but there are the various illness "walk-athons," and the occasional charity I've never even heard of. Once we contribute, we're usually locked into every subsequent year's event. One item of interest: I would say only 20-30% of the donations we make are followed up with a thank-you or other similar acknowledgement.

Just like in your personal life, your business charitable giving will be more effective and pleasing when you develop some guidelines for your gifts.

I want to give something back to the community that supports my small business, and frankly, I'd like some recognition for my donations!

Five Common Misconceptions about Business Giving, and Why They Aren't Necessarily True:

• Many business owners feel that their donation will be "too small" to matter, especially when compared to the much bigger and better-publicized gifts from large corporations.

Speaking as the founder and for many years, the executive director of a community-based nonprofit, I can assure you that no gift is too small. Why? When we apply to foundations for gifts, we often are asked how many donors we have. One of the tests set by the IRS for nonprofit status is the percentage of support that comes from the public. While we've never been asked how much each donor gave, we are sometimes asked for the total number of donors. So lots of donors – even $10 donors – means lots of community support, and that's very helpful to the organization.

• That he or she has to (or "should") give to everyone who asks in order to show support for the community (or for particular projects popular in town).

Following the principles in this book, business owners can and should give to the causes and projects that matter to them, their customers, their employees, even their families.

• That it is somehow less than noble to give with the main purpose being to get good exposure for the business.

In fact, all giving helps, no matter what the reason.

- **That they can give only cash or products.**

There are many, many ways to give, even when you own a business (see below).

- **If you give to one, you have to give to all.**

Not true at all! Having a giving policy means you can say "no."

How to Set Up an Effective Charitable Giving Program

You are a busy business owner. Setting up a giving program does not have to be difficult or complicated.

Larger businesses often set up a corporate foundation to handle their giving. In that case, they name a Board of Directors, and create a related but separate nonprofit organization, the purpose of which is to donate some of the profits of the corporation to charities they (or their employees, staff, vendors, or customers) choose. Most corporate foundations tend to give in their own communities or areas of operations. The shareholders can manage the foundation, but far more often, will hire an employee to do so on their behalf. Often, corporations expect some recognition for their gifts. And being involved in charitable giving is a commitment. One business owner, who also is very active in his community, says:

Is there such a thing as being too ambitious? Are there pitfalls? You bet! Running a business is stressful enough. Once you find the right charitable cause or project, you tend to get very passionate about it. It takes a lot of time.

Setting up a separate foundation likely requires too much paperwork, hands-on work, and legal requirements for the small business owner.

If that is the case, you simply can set up a Charitable Giving Program, and make donations directly to the charities of your choice from your business income. The arrangement is ideal for smaller businesses, those that are not incorporated, and owners who prefer a less formal arrangement with a lot less work.

Once you decide to make the gifts through a Charitable Giving Program, you then have another choice: you can pre-select recipients yourself, or you can open up your program to requests from community organizations.

If you decide the latter, how can you evaluate requests for funding? Here are the essential elements of a good request.[23] It should:

• Describe, simply and clearly, in one sentence, the purpose of the proposed project.

• Succinctly and clearly describe the problem the project is attempting to address. (It will not describe the ***organization's*** problem – such as a shortage of staff or funds – but the ***community's*** problem).

• Present a clear, compelling case for support, including what other solutions may have been tried, or what the "competition" has done, and why this project is needed.

• Describe in detail the project, the methods that will be used to deliver services, and what resources will be needed to do so.
• Include both a timetable for the project and delivery of services, as well as a description of the measures that will be used to evaluate the project's success.

---

[23] *Get That Grant*, op. cit.

• Finally, it will include a realistic and appropriate budget sufficient to complete the project.

In addition to what is presented to you in the request application, before you give a substantial donation, you likely also will want to meet the principals of the organization, to get a sense of who they are, and if you feel they will be good stewards of your gift.

If this is your wish, you have every right to ask for – and receive – public acknowledgement for your gift, either on the organization's website, or in another appropriate site.

Creative Ways to Give

If you decide not to accept direct requests from community organizations, you still have many viable options for giving:

- Donate your own expertise (such as offering accounting help for a new nonprofit) or services (such as reading to kindergarten children for an hour each week).

- Cover your employees' time for a day or a specific number of hours to volunteer for a cause you select (such as serving at a soup kitchen), where the entire company volunteers together.

- Give your employees a day (or a specific number of hours) off with pay to volunteer for the charity of their choice.

- Match the cash gifts your employees make to the charities of their choice, up to a certain limit predetermined by you.

- Partner with one organization, and make a capacity building grant, or a gift to start its endowment fund.

- Sponsor an event, such as a charity road race or a "Clean Up Our Park" Day.

- Start an ongoing community service project, like the dry cleaners that collect gently-used prom gowns, clean and repair them, and donate them to girls with limited resources.

- Create a Donor Advised Fund at your community foundation.

- Sponsor a Giving Circle.

- Involve your customers in giving. This can be as simple as prominently displaying a collection can for a charity on your counter, or asking everyone to donate a dollar for the "organization of the month" at checkout, to a more organized effort, such as giving customers a discount on new children's toys and puzzles when they bring in gently-used items their own children have outgrown (which you then donate).

Whichever vehicles you decide to use for your business giving, be sure they reflect your priorities and most important goals.

Consider:

If you own a small business, how might you incorporate giving as part of your business plan? Who will be involved? How can you best serve your community and get exposure for your business, if that is your goal?

Let no one be discouraged by the belief that there is nothing one person can do against the enormous array of the world's ills, misery, ignorance, and violence. Few will have the greatness to bend history, but each of us can work to change a small portion of events. And in the total of all those acts will be written the history of a generation.

- Robert F. Kennedy

Chapter Ten:
Encouraging Micro-Philanthropy

Once you have created and have been using your own Charitable Giving Plan, you may wish to share the pleasure of giving with others. If so, how can you encourage others to make their own gifts, or to become micro-philanthropists? Here are some ideas:

Make Charitable Giving Part of Life-Cycle Events and Other Occasions

Instead of a birthday present, I often make a gift in someone's honor. Now, it doesn't have to cost a lot, because the charity doesn't tell the amount of the gift to the recipient, just that you sent it. And they feel special, and it might even encourage them to do the same for someone else.

I made a gift in the name of my brother to the Juvenile Diabetes Foundation. He has diabetes, but he had never been involved with them. And then he in turn began to volunteer for them, and made lots of friends. So a gift can have far-reaching effects.

Just last year, as my extended family sat together in front of the tree at our mom and dad's house, having just opened dozens of gifts – that represented probably thousands of dollars *and hundreds of hours of time spent stressing, shopping, wrapping, and more stressing – we made a decision. From now on, only the school-aged children would get presents. The adults organized a system where everyone draws a name, and then donates $50 to a charity of the recipient's choosing. We think that's more in the spirit of Christmas than all the rampant commercialism.*

My friends and I are older now, and we don't need anything material. So I often donate to the Women's Fund nearest her in honor of a friend's birthday. I hope she'll do the same for another friend!

Don't Be Shy about "Going Public"

Many of us – often, but not always, women – are reluctant to let others know that we've made a gift to a specific cause. It's thought that "anonymous" givers most often are women, until one gets into the five-figure gift range, at which time anonymity may be an important consideration for every donor, both to ensure privacy and to avoid being hounded by every charity under the sun, who then would know of your capacity to give such a gift.

When you make a gift, especially an online gift to a charity that lists donors, consider foregoing modesty and anonymity by sharing your name and the amount of your gift. You'd be very surprised at how often that can inspire others to do the same.

There definitely is some peer pressure at work here. When I log onto a charity site to sponsor a friend in a road race, for example, and I see that another friend has given $50 – well, I might not be able to give that much, but I'm much more likely to give $25 than $10. I don't think anybody wants to be thought of as a cheapskate!

Sponsor Events That Bring in Small Donations from Others

When we heard that our friends across the county lost their home to a lightning strike, we took up a collection, and spread the word near and far. Even some folks who never met them, but who knew and trusted us, donated to help them rebuild.

Each year, our Girl Scout troop organizes a drive before the holidays to collect warm hats and mittens for needy children. People can bring in their items to our local bank, which displays an artificial tree with lots of clothespins – they just clip them right up – and that helps remind other bank customers to donate as well.

Challenge Others to Give by Matching Their Donations

For a one-time event or specific fund-raising campaign, you can effectively double your gift, by announcing (via social media or the organization's website or newsletter), that every gift – or every gift from a new donor – will be matched dollar (or a percentage) for dollar, up to your predetermined amount.

When our chapter did an end-of-the-year campaign, we especially wanted to encourage new members to give. I knew that most would be making small gifts, in the $10 to $25 range, so I spoke with the development officer ahead of time, and agreed to match all new donors' gifts up to a total of $500. We made the goal – and then some! So my $500 gift turned into more than $1,000, and we hope that many of these new donors will give again next year.

Choose One Small Problem to Address

One day, I was reading the newspaper and saw all the usual depressing stuff. On page three was a short article about *a small-town library in another part of the state that had been flooded. I thought, "Well, I can't solve the problems of the world, but here is something I **can** do." So with the help of a couple of friends, I organized a children's book drive. Eventually, a lot of children and their parents in the community got involved. We collected two truckloads of books and some monetary gifts – enough to almost fully re-stock the Children's Room.*

Share Your Enthusiasm – and This Book – with Others!

Encourage your friends to think about making their giving more effective and more enjoyable, by telling them how you find pleasure and satisfaction by giving. Do keep in mind, however, that as enthusiastic as you may be, about 20% of Americans – or one in five of your acquaintances – don't make charitable giving a priority, for a wide variety of personal reasons. Here are a few comments you might hear, as well as some possible responses:

- **I've just graduated and am still looking for my first job. I don't have anything to give.**

"If the right volunteer opportunity presented itself, could you find the time to donate two hours a week?"

- **I never give to charity. I use my money to help my own family, or friends who are down on their luck.**

"Great! Charity begins at home. And if your children, grandchildren, or friends need help, and you are able to give it, how fortunate for them and for you."

- **I'm working, but I don't have a lot left over – certainly nothing to give away.**

"I understand." I never try to convince someone that he or she has enough to give. If they think they don't, they don't. But depending on who it is, I might possibly remind them gently that 71% of the world's population lives on $10 or less a day.[24]

- **I just don't trust that my money will be used wisely.**

"It's good to be careful. And there are many ways you can – and should – vet an organization before you give. This book tells you how."

Identifying and Meeting a Need: Starting Your Own Nonprofit Organization

You read in Chapter Six about Zachary Hicks who, when he was just 13 years old, started a nonprofit to collect books for underprivileged children, which then became a huge success.

What if you'd like to start your own organization? My short answer to those who ask about this is: Don't. Not unless you absolutely can't help it. Creating a nonprofit can sound like a glamorous way to get your cause into the public eye and earn a living as its executive director. Not so. It's a lot of hard work and aggravation, and you certainly cannot count on earning a living wage, or even a salary – for at least the first five years.

But if there is a cause you love, and no one else to promote it but you, then go for it! Bear in mind, your new nonprofit will have to pass all the tests for giving described in this book, in order to secure funding sufficient to meet its goals.

As you begin, be certain to check your own state laws about how to get started. However, this should give you a general idea of what it takes:

---

[24] http://www.pewglobal.org/2015/07/08/a-global-middle-class-is-more-promise-than-reality

In addition to finding, recruiting, and training good, capable, and committed board members, you will be working with them to create a strategic plan, including crafting a mission statement, goals, and objectives, the implementation of which you will be leading.

You will be the Program Officer, responsible for creating, implementing, and evaluating the programs or services you intend to offer to the public. You will negotiate any possible difficulties with the public in terms of perception, understanding, and/or objections the community may have to your organization or the clientele it will serve.

You will be the Chief Development Officer, responsible for all aspects of fund development, including but not limited to these jobs: Annual Fund Director, Director of Major Gifts, Coordinator of Special Events, Grant Proposal Researcher and Writer, and Development Assistant, responsible for finding, applying for, tracking, and acknowledging all gifts, including required reporting, and finding the right development software package for your needs. And eventually, down the road a bit, you'll also be the Endowment Fund Manager.

You will be Chief Marketing Officer, in charge of creating a brand for your new nonprofit, getting the name and mission in front of the public, networking with other nonprofit organizations and likely also with community organizations such as the local Chamber of Commerce, your city or county business associations, and so on.

You also will be the contact for all media inquiries about your organization, and will be writing, editing, and sending out press releases on a regular basis as required. You will take every opportunity to write Letters to the Editor to help promote your organization's mission, as appropriate. You will commission or design a logo and stationery package for your organization, find and hire a printer, website designer, and webmaster, if you are not skilled at these tasks, plus an IT team who will return your calls promptly in case of a technical emergency.

You will be reading nonstop about trends and developments in your field, so that your conversations with reporters and with potential funders reflect the most current knowledge. You'll be networking with colleagues to create opportunities for collaborative ventures, so very critical in today's funding climate.

You will be the Office Manager: responsible for finding, negotiating rent on, and upkeep of office space, procuring equipment and supplies, keeping meticulous books (which, except for the names of donors, must be open to the public at all times), filing necessary paperwork with your state Attorney General's office yearly, including any special permits your state may require, plus the forms required by the IRS, and perhaps also by your city or town.

You'll be the one to empty the trash cans at night and sweep the floors. You will be answering phone calls and emails and writing thank you notes for donations and newspaper stories.

You will be recruiting, managing, and evaluating any staff and/or volunteers, and, in the case of hired staff, responsible for payroll, choosing benefits, reviews, and creating a personnel policy and handbook.

If you are working alone, then you will be doing all of the above minus the staff and volunteers. And, as stated above, you should always plan on having another source of income for at least the first five years of operations.

All this notwithstanding, if you have a zeal for your mission and are willing to roll up your sleeves and give it everything you've got, then go for it!

The Power of Our Collective Micro-Philanthropy

When we think strategically about how to make charitable gifts, and join our gifts with others', we can make enormous changes. Micro-philanthropy has a long history. Some of the more notable efforts include:

The March of Dimes

Created in 1938, driven by President Franklin Delano Roosevelt, who had polio and was keenly interested in finding a cure, The National Foundation for Infantile Paralysis, (the March of Dimes), sought to involve the public and alleviate fear of the disease by engaging the entire country in giving micro-donations. Collections of coins were made in schools, religious congregations, community organizations, and even in movie theaters. Everyone who was able to do so contributed to beat the disease that terrified the whole country. In 1939, $1.8 million was raised in dimes and dollar bills. In 1955, $67 million was raised. These funds served to support Dr. Jonas Salk's successful research, which led to the development of a vaccine for polio.

When the tested, approved vaccine was finally announced to the public on April 12, 1955, the country's reaction was one of euphoria. In the words of cultural anthropologist Heather Wood Ion: "More than a scientific achievement, the vaccine was a folk victory, an occasion of pride and jubilation. A contagion of love swept the world." Dr. Jonas Salk himself continued to promote an "epidemic of health"[25] and he refused to patent or profit from his work.

---

[25] Munnecke, Tom, and Wood-Ion, Heather, "Creating an Epidemic of Health," US Medicine Magazine, Washington, DC August 1995, cited in Tom Munnecke and Heather Wood Ion. "Towards a Model of Micro Philanthropy" May 21, 2002.

UNICEF

In December, 1946, the United Nations Children's Emergency Fund (UNICEF) was created to provide food, clothing, and health care to European children who were facing disease and famine after World War II. UNICEF later expanded its mission to include children's protection; nutrition; education, including teacher training and supplies for classrooms; as well as human rights.[26]

Seventy years later, a portion of UNICEF's funds still comes from the door-to-door efforts of school children, who carry the iconic orange collection boxes on Halloween, along with their candy collection bags. For four generations of American children, "Trick or Treat for UNICEF" was their first exposure to micro-philanthropy.

Crowdfunding

Crowdfunding – the concept of many pooled small donations to fund a common venture – has a very long history, dating back hundreds of years, and including such popular efforts as War Bonds.

In 1971, with the Concert for Bangladesh, and then Band Aid and Live Aid, a new era of crowdfunding was born: the charity concert. And with it began the collaboration of technology and philanthropy. From those concerts to the 2014 Ice Bucket Challenge to raise funds for ALS, "Activism is now a computer mouse away."[27]

---

[26] www.unicef.org.
[27] Clyde Haberman, "Philanthropy That Comes From a Click", Retro Report. *NY Times*, November 13, 2016.

First used to help fund start-up businesses and artistic projects such as films and other visual and performing arts, internet crowdfunding has added an interesting new dimension to micro-philanthropy, almost revolutionizing the way today's nonprofits raise funds.

With varying areas of interest, from arts organizations to human rights causes, any nonprofit that is seeking to raise its visibility, expand and engage its network and pool of donors and volunteers, and attract foundations and corporate sponsors, can use sites such as CrowdRise, Indiegogo, GoFundMe, and Kickstarter, which now have become trusted vehicles for micro-philanthropy.

According to Wikipedia, more than $34 billion was raised via crowdfunding in 2015 for a wide variety of causes, many of them nonprofits.

The Huge Transfer of Wealth Has Begun

According to researchers at Boston College, an estimated $59 trillion "divided among heirs, charities, estate taxes and estate closing costs," have passed and will pass to the next generations between 2007 and 2061: the "greatest wealth transfer in U.S. history," with heirs receiving $36 trillion.[28]

And, although it is true that most of us could use a few extra dollars, presumably none of that $36 trillion is needed for our basic survival (since we don't have it now) and therefore could be tapped as a source for additional charitable giving – both for us and for our children and grandchildren.

---

[28] John J. Havens and Paul G. Schervish, "A Golden Age of Philanthropy Still Beckons: National Wealth Transfer and Potential for Philanthropy." The Center on Wealth and Philanthropy, Boston College, 2014.

A Vision for Our Future

With carefully organized, focused giving, consider what we could do **right now** with the nearly $300 billion individuals donated last year in the U.S. alone. That's a lot of new day care centers, more funding for medical research, support for developing new technology, and greatly expanded environmental action. It could mean fully stocked food pantries, accessible art museums, well-paid teachers and schools functioning optimally, as well as an ample safety net for our most vulnerable populations.

When we thoughtfully consider how to give our money away, and create a proactive Charitable Giving Plan, our personal and collective micro-philanthropy can and will have far-reaching effects on how our society survives into the next generations.

What are you going to do with the change in **your** pocket?

Acknowledgements

My gratitude to:

Carla C. Cataldo and Nancy Haverstock, for kind permission to use here some of our previous collaborative work.

Zachary Hicks, Nadine Nesbitt, Rev. Maddie Sifantus, and the many anonymous others who very graciously shared their stories and experiences.

Michael Brian Murphy, for careful editing.

Sandra Pirie-St. Amour, for the delightful cover illustration.

Ray Ringston of Ringston Media, for reinventing the wheel.

Janet Rosen, for suggesting the title many years ago.

First readers Becky Sarah, Rita Shapiro, A. Rae Simpson, and Gil Wolin, for astute, helpful, and kind comments.

Angela and Richard Hoy, and the entire team at BookLocker, for providing the platform for this work.

The many clients, workshop participants, and nonprofit colleagues with whom I've had the privilege to work, for expanding my vision of what it means to be generous.

My family, for continual support, love, and forbearance.

And to you, the reader, for being open to learning more about how to make your giving more meaningful and more pleasurable.